11-8-65

youth ventures
toward a vital church

youth ventures
toward a vital church

SHEILA D. WOODS

ABINGDON PRESS
new york • nashville

YOUTH VENTURES TOWARD A VITAL CHURCH

Copyright © 1965 by Abingdon Press

All rights in this book are reserved.

Library of Congress Catalog Card Number: 65-21978

SET UP, PRINTED, AND BOUND BY THE PARTHENON PRESS, AT NASHVILLE, TENNESSEE, UNITED STATES OF AMERICA

TO THE IONA COMMUNITY

A New People Have Emerged

The church is renewed.
Not sometime. Not tomorrow.
The victory is now.
Awakening forces
struggling for half a hundred years
against odds unbelievable
have swept the day. The battle is sure,
though many are yet to die in making manifest
the victory.
A swelling tide is rising and rolling
within, throughout, and across the land.
The Gospel is recovered,
the laity are rising up.
The task is coming clear,
a new image of ecclesia is given.
The people of God arise.
No man nor power can turn them back,
no guilt ridden pharisee
no sentimental dreamer of the past
no intellectual reductionist
no blind leader of the blind
however numerous, however strong, however
entrenched.
The axe is laid at the root.
The angels sing. Humble waiters on the hills
are hearing their song.
This is the knocking. The renewed church.
Awake, arise ye peculiar ones.
Be of good courage. Dare to wax bold, risking all.
the kingdom is yours.
Now is the time,
It is our father's house.
Christmas has come.

Christmastide
Nineteen Sixty Four

(Published by the Directors and Faculty of the Ecumenical Institute, Chicago. Used by permission.)

ACKNOWLEDGMENT

I would like to express my sincere thanks to Mrs. Paul S. Wright, who compiled and typed the index—a most arduous job.

CONTENTS

Introduction 13

Chapter   I What on Earth Is a Church?

1. God Is Not a Captive in Church—
   Thank God! 21
2. Think of a Church—Our Church 24
3. On Going to Church 26
4. Why I Go to Church 29
5. Always the Stiff-necked People 32
6. A New Church in a New Town 36
7. A Church in the Inner City 37
8. The Charred Cross 40
9. What Is the Shape of the Church for the
   World of Tomorrow? 42
10. Additional Worship Resources 44

Chapter   II   Come Out, Come Out, Wherever You Are!

1. Glory to God in the High St. 47
2. The Godforsaken People 49
3. Arise, Go to Nineveh—I Mean Chicago 52
4. "I Ain't Got No Use for the Church!. 55
5. God's Switchboard Operators 58
6. The Case of the Church *v.* the
   Department of Housing 61
7. The Church in Their House 63
8. The Church Among the Carrots 65
9. Additional Worship Resources 67

Chapter   III   Keep My Brother?

1. Seeing the Unseen 70
2. We Need a "Good Samaritan" Law! 72
3. A Cup of Cold Water 75
4. An Extra Pair of Jeans 77
5. Keep My Brother? Who Is He? 79
6. The Church Is for Anybody 82
7. Additional Worship Resources 84

Chapter   IV   No Man Is Innocent of Hate

1. What Is Hate? 87
2. Aftermath of an Assassination 89
3. Ten Commandments on How Best to
   Undermine America 92
4. The Root of Bitterness 93
5. Was Anne Frank's Father Apathetic? 96
6. We Do Not Make Room 99
7. The Disgrace of Silence 101
8. Casting Black and White Stones 105
9. Additional Worship Resources 108

Chapter V **The Changing Patterns of Work**

1. Be Worthy of Your Hire 111
2. The Meaning of Work 113
3. September 116
4. On Being a "Proper Christian" 119
5. Poverty? Survival of the Fittest, You Know! . . 121
6. Money, Money, Money! 124
7. The Church and PR 126
8. Time Off—For What? 129
9. Additional Worship Resources 132

Chapter VI **Living out on a Limb**

1. Is There a Time of Religious Hibernation? . . . 135
2. "Christians" Who Play It Cool 137
3. Sexplosion 140
4. The Ten Commandments Today 142
5. Thou Shalt Get by with It 146
6. The Times Call for Men Who Dare 149
7. God's Fireweed 152
8. The Church of the Saviour,
   Washington, D. C. 155
9. Some New Disciplines Within the Church . . . 158

Chapter VII **Christianity═Community**

1. Man Is Alone—Yet No Man Is Alone 162
2. The Confusions of Mary and Martha 164
3. Members of the Household of God 167
4. 400,000 Sang Together at the Kirchentag 169
5. A Bridge Between the Church
   and the World 172
6. The Iona Community 176
7. Taizé—and Understanding Between
   all Christians 179
8. Additional Worship Resources 182

Chapter VIII   **Glory to God in the Highest**

     1.   What Is This Thing Called Glory? 184

     2.   Praise God from Whom All Blessings Flow ...186

     3.   The Wonders of God's World 189

     4.   What Is Worship? 192

     5.   The Meaning of Holy Communion 194

     6.   A Table with a Roof Over It 197

     7.   Additional Worship Resources 199

Chapter IX   **Opportunities for Action by Comfortable Christians**

     1.   Action in the World Today 204

     2.   What Can You Do? 219

     3.   Other Useful Addresses 221

Notes 223

Bibliography 231

Index 235

INTRODUCTION

During the recent troubles in Mississippi a minister wrote, "We serve as a steeple sticking up into the fog." [1] He was referring to the many hundreds of ministers and laymen of all denominations, working to clear an atmosphere of hate, fear, and suspicion.

It was also a good description of the new image of the church that is beginning to emerge, at last. For too long those who have thought about steeples at all have seen them as symbols of fingers pointing to heaven, when they should have been beacons shining on men below, where the work of the Christian is waiting to be done.

The changes in the world today are taking place at a greater rate of speed than ever before in history. Man has needed the anchor of faith to maintain his equilibrium, but when he has turned to the church for help, its people have seemed to be preoccupied with committees, programs, and dinners, and something called the "spiritual life," which was inclined to make the outsider feel not quite good enough—as if he had used the wrong bleach to wash away his sins. The church condemned him for drifting away, but did not seem to wonder if *it* might not have been responsible for the drifting!

Those who, as Christians, gave help to the needy in the world, felt it was also their duty to try to bring these people "into the fold"; or they had failed. True, some of our finest men and women have served in our churches, in the mission fields at home and in foreign countries and have attracted others to Christ through sheer, selfless devotion. But they have been looked on as the chosen few and considered a little unworldly. For many years now the ordinary man-in-the-church has been becoming more and more embarrassed by words like "evangelism," "missionary," and "witness." Not that there is anything wrong with these words, but the use of them and application of them to modern situations have been as irrelevant as an oil lamp instead of electricity, or a horse and buggy instead of a turbojet.

This irrelevance of the church to the problems of man in contemporary life has been the greatest cause of a need for renewal. It has been the biggest stumbling block for each young person as he has made his commitment to Christ, eagerly expecting to join the life of the church and *do* something. Instead he has felt out of place, been considered too young for responsibility or service, and kept in the same old pattern of youth fellowship meetings.

Whether he went on to college, to a job, to marriage, to a term in the armed services—the church seemed irrelevant to whatever he was doing. It did not understand his language, have any interest in his interests—his desire to be a part of the church and do something worthwhile. As one boy put it, "It's as if the church is trying to insist that we keep on wearing 'baggy' pants when everyone wears the 'pegged' kind nowadays. They don't seem to listen, so we just give up and don't come back."

Now, radical changes are taking place. The church is venturing into factories and stores, politics and social issues, cafés and homes, hospitals and prisons—meeting men and women where they are. In some areas Christians have gone much further than they ever anticipated or dreamed—as in the civil rights movement. With glad relief they hear they are to help anyone, in any way possible, regardless of whether that person ever sets foot in a church as the result of being helped. (The hope is that they will ask "Why are you doing this for me? What's the church all about, anyway?" And *then* the Christian can give his answer.)

There is nothing new in all this. Christ emphasized the role of servant, and rebuked the Pharisees for their ingrowing ritual and pious self-righteousness.

As in all new ventures there are extremists; those who would wipe out the clergy, and consider the local church building as unnecessary. The clergy and the institutional church will *always* be needed, but instead of the people gathering in a church building, they will gather for training and encouragement before being sent back outside again! Now, as never before, the lay people are needed to do many of the tasks that were previously left to the minister or clergy.

As Hans Margull has said, we must change our local churches from " 'come-structures' to 'go-structures.' "

The heart of the church is its worship, where men come together to praise God, to confess their failures, to be renewed through forgiveness, to hear God's Word, and go out into the world again as the servants of all men, loving and serving, as Christ loved and served.

This renewal of the church is the work of God, not of men. The church may wither on the vine through the fault of men, but it does not die; it flowers again in a new way. We look for the signs of this, and we follow. Today they seem to be seen in a call for deeper commitment and obedience, for a different interpretation of that word "evangelism," for a realization that the church *is* "mission," and for a new task for the layman. This flower of renewal can be seen most clearly in the hearts of our cities, among the poor and wretched. Here new ways of worship are being tried that will have meaning for those who live there. George W. Webber, who has worked in East Harlem Protestant Parish in New York City for many years, has written:

"It is hard to write about our worship life, for inevitably we confuse our vision of what ought to be happening or what we want to happen with the reality that God is willing to grant to us. We can only pray that in our freedom to seek new patterns of worship we shall learn to listen and obey God, for surely He is here among the needs and problems of our community, calling us to join Christ who is always to be found wherever there is poverty and blindness and captivity and oppression." [2]

These words can apply, not only to the search for new patterns of worship, to the search for new forms of Christian living, but in our study of the Bible which gives direction to our lives. Perhaps it is this word "direction" that has been missing, and has made the church "behind the times." The people of the church have always studied the Bible closely, but more for the memorization and understanding of its contents, than in the search for its directions to men. Christians should live *in response to* these directions, and if they had, they would never have stayed inside their church buildings, but gone out long ago into the world—where Christ is, ahead of them.

WHAT IS THE PURPOSE OF THIS BOOK?

1. To inform youth of the many new ventures of the church today as it goes back into the world.
2. To see these ventures in the light of God's Word in the Bible, when youth meets to worship.
3. To discuss these ventures, directly following worship, with the avowed intent of taking some form of action or service.
4. To dedicate these decisions in prayer.

Each chapter of the book explores some area of church renewal, through a series of topics. Each topic contains:
   a. Scripture
   b. Reading
   c. Suggestions for discussion and action
   d. Prayer

Extra scripture, prayers, and suggested hymns are also given at the end of each chapter.

It is not suggested that these four elements form a service of worship. Each group will have its own denominational service book and select other parts of worship, depending on the length of the service.

This skeletal foundation will allow freedom of choice in the preparation of the service and the opportunity to explore some new forms of prayer and song, according to the nature and needs of the group.

These services have no connection whatsoever with the service of Sunday worship for the congregation, led by an ordained minister. They are intended for the times when youth meet together in worship, led by one or two of their members.

Such services are often a hodge-podge of unrelated items based on "hymns people like best," the leader's "favorite Scripture," and a prayer either of the kind that should be used in personal prayer or in language that is archaic.

The words "order of service" are familiar. They do not refer to a command, or the order in which the parts of worship fall. "Order" comes from the Latin *ordo*, "arrangement," "order." And these "arrangements" should be carefully planned ahead of time, for we do not worship God carelessly.

Among the "arrangements," be sure to have a leader or a group prepared to lead the discussion, preferably not the person who has been the reader. In many instances you may want to invite your minister or other outside speakers to take part in the discussion. In the Bibliography you will find books that may help, as well as a list of audio-visual resources on the renewal of the church.

To allow time for "discussion and action," a brief service will be best. Perhaps opening with the words "let us worship God," which will immediately indicate that worship has begun and that we worship *together*. Or a hymn of praise and adoration could be used. A prayer of confession could follow this, or come after the reading (in which case it should be brief and written by the leader, with direct relationship to the subject). The prayer given at the end of each topic is merely a suggestion, and another may have to be substituted if the discussion takes off in a direction that might make it irrelevant.

Music is one of the biggest problems when small groups meet to worship. Most people love to sing, but fewer and fewer people are capable of playing the piano (or organ) sufficiently well enough to give a good supportive accompaniment. The number of hymns known by a group is small, and in their resistance to learn new ones the group can be downright stubborn! [3]

If your church has a tape recorder, you might try the experiment of making a collection of recordings of hymns, played by your church organist—just as he would for a church service, with the introductory lines, and the number of verses required. Have the machine behind the group, and control the volume so that it inspires your group to join in, instead of drowning them out! New hymns can be added to the collection with this same method.

WHAT ABOUT CHAPTER IX
—OPPORTUNITIES FOR ACTION BY
COMFORTABLE CHRISTIANS?

This will not be easy! The resistance and difficulties that confront Christians when they come out of their churches are part of the "fog" referred to in the first paragraph of this introduction. Too many steeples are submerged in that fog.

A great majority of the American people today consider they are "Christian" in rather the same unthinking way that they get out to vote, believe in a balanced diet, and tell the truth when possible and convenient. They feel that the words "under God" in the Pledge of Allegiance are like carrying an umbrella in case it rains. They may even belong to a particular denomination, joining it as they join the local P.T.A., garden club, or men's club. They tolerate those who are known as "active" members of a church so long as they keep their ideas inside that church building, preferably on a Sunday. The expressions of a Christian outside the building may be met with "we understand your personal feelings and respect them, but in the world today we have to be realistic!" Or "The church has no business meddling in politics."

The Christian must become aware of the needs and the sufferings of all people and do something about them, whether it be the young girl across the street who has become pregnant, the boy who is a drug addict, or the Appalachian baby dying of starvation. The Christian needs to look at life through bifocal lens, becoming sensitive to needs close at hand and far away.

Chapter IX will give you a bird's-eye view of some of the things being done, some that are waiting to be done, with many addresses for those who want to get started on some form of service and action. After reading each section you should turn to Chapter IX if you wish to learn more about new ideas for church action.

Your aim is to listen, discuss, and act in the light of God's Word, praying for his grace that you may venture along the path toward a more vital church.

WHAT ON EARTH *IS* A CHURCH?

1. GOD IS NOT A CAPTIVE
IN CHURCH—THANK GOD!

Scripture: Mark 7:1-9 ("This people honors me with their lips.")

Reading:

A man attended the 1961 North American Youth Assembly at Ann Arbor, Michigan. The Assembly, which lasted a week, drew two thousand young people from forty denominations. The man was scheduled to be the last speaker, and as the time drew near he grew restless. He wrote a letter to friends:

"I have been sitting here in my air-conditioned room, sipping coffee and meditating about what to say to these people. But for one or two intrusions, this is a prosaic, churchy meeting. The bunting and the theatrics do not conceal the fact that the gospel is treated here with embarrassment and caution, as it is in most congregations.

"The amenities are too comfortable, though I am now accustomed to accepting them with a show of grace. The people are too clean—and they have all recently eaten." [1]

The speaker was William Stringfellow, and he lived at that time in a tenement in East Harlem. Upon graduation from Harvard Law School he chose to set up practice among the desperately poor, rather than in a district where success and wealth might come easily. Most of his clients were Puerto Ricans and Negroes. He helped them with their legal problems, and above all he helped them with their struggle to live.

Why did William Stringfellow choose to work there? He felt that this was what God wanted him to do. This does not mean he feels that everyone should choose poverty as a Christian vocation, nor does he feel there is any virtue in doing so. He *does* feel that every Christian should read the Bible, listen to what it says to him, and do it.

In his speech to the Youth Assembly he said:

"What Christians are faced with, I suggest, is churches which—at every echelon of their being: Sunday school, youth fellowships vestries and sessions, agencies, councils, denominations, congregations and parishes, women's work, rummage sales, bingo games and coffee hours, sermons, seminaries, boy scouts, choirs, and dial-a-prayers, pseudo-Gothic architecture, segregated premises, effete or effeminate images of Jesus, and grossly overstaffed bureaucracies—are to a great extent separated from the world, . . . so that pretty soon they think they don't have to care about the world any more since they are so much consumed in caring for themselves.

"Yet it is when and where the churches are most estranged from the common life of the world that the churches are most worldly. The separation of the churches from the world—the superstition that the gospel is isolated from ordinary, everyday life—is the same thing as estrangement from Christ. Where the churches do not care for the world, they do not really care for Christ. . . .

"God is not a captive in church—thank God! God is his own witness in this world: in every time and place, in that which seems

22

to our blindness good and worthy to be praised and in that which seems to our blindness evil and possessed of death. In his Word the world was made, and in all the world his Word resides, and there is no excuse for those who do not honor him as God." [2]

Suggestions for Discussion and Action:

Read the scripture again. Then relate it to the reading you have just heard. What does it say to your group, in your particular church? (Don't start criticizing the church as a whole, that's too easy! Be specific and honest.)

Does your group tend to be like some secret society? Christians are no longer thrown to the lions, why do they keep to themselves so much?

It has been suggested that churches might break down some of this exclusiveness by meeting in other places than the church building, not because they are not suitable, but to demonstrate that the church belongs to the community as a whole. What do you think of this idea? "If there were less distinction between the things that could and the things that could not be done in a church hall and a real interchange of place of meeting, there would be more of a sense that people matter more than activities and that all the people of the neighborhood belong to the church, at least in the eyes of the church and in its care." [3]

What action is your group going to take?

Prayer:

"Stir up in thy church compassion and understanding for all people caught in compromise and tension between their faith and their work. Let it be so much in the world that none may accuse it of being indifferent to the daily struggle, yet so devoted to thy Kingdom that it can forthrightly declare the good news of reconciliation through Jesus Christ our Lord. In his name we pray. Amen." [4]

2. THINK OF A CHURCH—OUR CHURCH

Scripture: Col. 3:12-17 ("Do everything in the name of the Lord Jesus.")

Reading:

First Reader: "Think of a church . . .

Second Reader: "Perhaps, our church, . . . on a Sunday morning.

"Think of our church building . . . of the piece of land on which it stands, and the length of time it has stood there.

"Think of the familiar touch of its seats, of the place where the light streams in like a long ladder; of its own particular smell of floor polish and flowers; of the rustle and beginning of music as the choir comes in; of the hymnals, and the offering plate, and the hands of those who pass it to us.

"Think of our pastor, our preacher, our minister, as he stands in the pulpit, his fingers turning the pages of the Bible before he begins to read; his voice, his expression, his particular job in this particular building with these people.

First Reader: "Doing what? What is he doing here? What are all these people doing here? The butcher and the banker, the old lady in her dateless dress, the truck driver, the teacher, the soldier home on leave, the little boy doodling on his Sunday school paper, the waitress from the cafe on Main Street, the doctor and the farmer;

widows and widowers, husbands and wives,
those from a big family, those who live alone,
engaged couples, those going steady,
groups of boys, groups of girls,
small children, and an occasional baby.

"What on earth are they all doing here on a Sunday morning? All mixed up together, all dressed up with neckties and gloves, rustling petticoats and outlandish hats.

"What on earth are they all doing here on a Sunday morning

24

when they could have slept late, had another cup of coffee, gone out to play golf, mowed the lawn, played with dolls or guns, or even watched television?

Second Reader: "Who are they, and why are they here?

First Reader: "Why?

Second Reader: "Think of the other churches around us, the brick and the wood, the old and weathered, the new and strange, those with crosses and steeples and altars and bells and choirs.

"Those with no music at all.

"Those who do not even meet on a Sunday.

"Think of them . . . spread across the land.

"Squeezed between skyscrapers in the deep cities; out on the wide prairie squeezed between the wheat fields; encircled with well-placed shrubs and bordered by neat suburbs; surrounded by trees; up in the mountains; powdered with dust from the desert; and sprayed with salt from the sea.

"Think of them.

"All across our country, up into Canada and the Far North; down through Mexico and the islands of the Carribbean; farther down through the vast countries of South America; down to the Horn around which many of our ancestors came with their beds and boxes and Bibles; out to the East and out to the West, all around the world.

"So many people and so many churches.

First Reader: "Why do people go to church?" [5]

Suggestions for Discussion and Action:

Read the selected scripture again.

Do this passage and the reading you have just heard describe your church?

After all, *is* it "your" church?

If your group still lives at home, what part does everyone play in the life of the church? What *is* the "life of the church"? Do you know what kind of teaching is used in the kindergarten, the purpose of the women's meetings, how the church spends its money, and what your church "stands for"? If you feel, after free discussion, that you are not too sure what a church is and what it should be, *what are you going to do about it?*

If you are away from home, maybe at college, do you still feel a part of the church where you hold membership? When you go to another church, how do you feel? Do you have a greater understanding of your own denomination, or do you feel strange because it is not like "the church back home"? Or, did you feel better able to participate because it was *not* like "the church back home"?

Do you feel you know the beliefs and purposes of your own denomination, and of Christianity at large? If not, *what are you going to do about it?*

Throw it away, as part of your childhood?

Delve into it, as part of your adulthood?

Some possible actions are—exploring, reading, praying, listening, thinking, deciding, maybe to take part in some work related to the church which is quite new to you.

Prayer:

Lord God, we come before you humbly, but with an inquiring and critical mind, as we try to know your church and become a part of it. If we tear down, help us to build up. If we discover inadequacies, help us to discover our own inadequacies too. Above all, O God, help us to remember that this is your church. Help us to listen for the way you would have us go; and give us the strength to do it, through the knowledge of the love of thy Son, Jesus Christ. Amen.

3. ON GOING TO CHURCH

Scripture: Eph. 3:14-21 ("To him be glory in the church.")

Reading:

"Church-going is a tricky thing for Christians to discuss dispassionately. It arouses very strong feelings of loyalty and disloyalty, of guilt and insecurity. . . .

"Let us consider, briefly, what a local church ought to be like, as the local embodiment of the Love of Christ for His world. It must show, in everything it does, from its public worship to its training about how its members spend their incomes, a sense of *serving*—of serving, not even primarily other church members, but the people in the neighborhood outside the congregation, for whom our Lord died. We do not worship a God who is some kind of oriental despot, before whom we must grovel like condemned slaves (and mutter the Name of Jesus so that we may be let off). We worship a God who Himself washed people's dirty feet, and this is why we do Him reverence. We must not be concerned for the whiter than white purity of our souls (for then we stand in terrible danger of losing them), we must walk boldly and steadily (and regularly each Monday morning, which is harder) into the compromising situations of local politics, of shopkeeping, of buying and selling and hiring and firing—for there we shall find our Lord, in the hospitals and prisons and slums and unemployment queues of our time. He is wherever we find 'the least of these our brethren.' In short, a local church which dares to call itself Christian must be a genuine community of people determined to work out together a life of sacrificial love. . . .

"At this point a good many readers may be a bit puzzled, and a few distinctly angry. 'The Church is not just a social service institution,' they are muttering. 'What about the worship of Almighty God? And when you say that the services seem irrelevant, surely this is because the casual droppers-in to services haven't learnt the language. If they would take the trouble to understand our magnificent prayer book (or Methodist hymns, or what have you) they would see the importance of divine worship and of Christian teaching. . . .'

"To some extent this is true. . . . There are one or two things which should be found in any church service in 1963. One is, of course, a certain amount of the traditional—to link us deliberately with the past . . . but not throughout the service, as if to give us the sense of attending some kind of an historical pageant. . . .

"We ought to say to the non-churchgoing Christian: 'Yes, worship together is an essential part of the Christian life.' But we cannot say: 'You must learn to do what we have always done.' We must add: 'We have become far too set in our ways. Tell us frankly what you don't understand. Help us to find the symbols and words which fit this day and age. And teach us, above all, to remember our neighbours outside the church walls, whom we must serve as serving God Himself.' " [6]

Suggestions for Discussion and Action:

Read the selected scripture again.

These verses seem to describe parts of a worship service. List these parts and discuss them (such as "bow," "strengthened," "to him be the glory").

What about the comments in the reading you have just heard? Such as, "One or two things should be found in any church service . . . to link us deliberately with the past," and "But . . . not to give us the sense of attending some kind of historical pageant." How do you feel about this? What is the difference between a service led by a minister, and one led by a member of your own group? (See the Introduction for some help on this.)

How is your group "as the church" when scattered on a Monday morning? How would you explain, in words or actions, how the church should be on a Monday morning?

Plan, as a group, some new way in which you can walk into a difficult situation and serve your neighbor. Choose one from those mentioned in the reading. If you can't find one, you should be worried! If you think you are doing all these things anyway, you should be even more worried!

Prayer:

Lord God, help us to find words and symbols of worship relevant to our living in the world today. Help us to remember that the word "neighbor" is also a symbol for anyone and everyone with whom we come in contact, in any place; and teach us to know how to serve our neighbor as serving God himself; and to him be the glory in the church, through Jesus Christ. Amen.

4. WHY I GO TO CHURCH

Scripture: Ps. 122:1 ("Let us go to the house of the Lord.")

Reading:

First Reader: Some years ago John Turner, a University of Oregon student, charged that the church was not giving his generation a challenge or a cause.[7] This inspired the Methodist magazine *Together* to ask for essays on the topic, "Why I go to church." The readings that follow are excerpts from the essays of the two co-winners.

Second Reader: Jo Chapman, then at the University of California, wrote:

"The friend of a television star once described him as a 'very religious person,' but admitted that the actor didn't go to church often. We've all heard similar statements by people who feel they don't need to go to church to be Christians. 'I don't need to go to church,' they say. 'I can worship God in the forest (or in the mountains, or on city streets, or in the home).'

"This type of thinking is akin to that of many churchgoers who say, in effect: 'It's a nice place to visit, but I wouldn't want to make it a habit.' Obviously, many believers feel the church is unnecessary. Some even denounce the church as an evil in itself which should change its structure or be done away with altogether.

"Yet, it isn't violent criticism which disturbs young people who attend church regularly. Any institution which can't bear criticism is unworthy of existence. More unsettling is the indifference of those considered Christians.

"Frankly, we are puzzled by those who make annual excursions to the church on Christmas or Easter to yawn their way through sermons, sit unmoved by the music, and survey their surroundings with obvious boredom. Perhaps the sermons are dull, the music trite or off key, and the surroundings colorless. But why don't these people do something about it? They seem to feel no compulsion to inject spirit and vitality into the worship of God.

"Before we decry the attitude of these people, we must make sure that we are not among them. We must ask ourselves: Why do I go to church? What does it really mean to me? Is it a necessary part of my life?" [8]

First Reader: Richard Henze, then at Evansville College, Indiana, wrote:

"Why do I go to church? I really never thought about it much. I was brought up in the church, and my parents and my friends go to church. Why shouldn't I go? . . .

"My life runs along pretty smoothly, and sometimes I let whole days go by without even thinking of God. I have friends, good health, and enough money to buy what I want. I don't have to drive through the slums to get to work or school. Why should I weight myself down with thoughts of sin, death, and damnation? . . .

"I don't remember much from the sermons I've heard, but at least I don't sleep through them the way a lot of people do. Even though my attention wanders, I do stay awake. I look around a lot at the girls. But then, I'm only 21, and at that age men do tend to look at the girls.

"Sometimes I just sit there and wonder about these girls. Is church improving their characters, or merely giving them exposure and increased social contacts? Are they getting any good out of the service itself? I realize I don't always get much out of it myself.

But I have a good feeling when I leave. I shake hands with the minister, and with most of the people too. I like people.

"Sometimes, of course, I think about sin and it worries me. I've heard lots about sin. Some people seem to think almost everything is a sin, others don't seem to think anything is. I know I commit some sins, but I also know I couldn't avoid them all. I just try to side-step the things I feel are wrong and get on the best I can. I don't argue about religion, and I stay out of trouble. If I can, I guess I'll go on like this. . . .

"Why do I go to church, then? That's a difficult question, and I don't have many definite answers to give. Oh, I go for the fellowship and to watch the girls, but I could find those some place else. There's more to it than that. When I think about it, I think it must be the story I hear there. I can find strength and hope in all the people gathered together, wanting and believing.

"It doesn't seem possible that all the evil gathered in a church on Sunday morning could be forgiven. Yet it must be, or nothing is possible. There is more than fellowship at work there, if I could just explain it. There is hope that our sins and suffering will end not in oblivion, but in redemption and life beyond death. There is a key that can be found nowhere else to life, meaning, and salvation. This is what I seek, and I know I must find it in the church. It can be found nowhere else." [9]

Suggestions for Discussion and Action:

Most churches keep files of their magazines. See if you can borrow the two issues of *Together*. This can be an ecumenical project if you are not a Methodist!

Read the scripture again.

With the material in the magazines, and open discussion, prepare, for some future date, to discuss the issue "Are We in Danger of Becoming Comfortable Christians in Comfortable Churches?"

If this is found to be true, what action will you be prepared to take to remedy the situation?

If this is found to be untrue, how can you further prove your point and make it known to others, inside and out of the church?

Prayer:

"O Lord, let us not live to be useless; for Christ's sake. Amen." [10]

5. ALWAYS THE STIFF-NECKED PEOPLE

Scripture: I Cor. 10:1-6 ("With most of them God was not pleased.")

Reading:

First Reader: Although the motion picture industry has been criticized for some of its interpretation of the Old Testament, few can deny that with the wide screens and good color of today, it has been able to catch some of the vitality and boldness of the children of Israel. They were a people called by God, and he had endless patience with them. The Old Testament is full of accounts of their turning away from him, of his forgiveness and offer of another chance. To us, their memories seem so short. Moses had only to climb a mountain, and there they were, dancing around a golden calf again! The description of their somewhat bloodthirsty lives is highlighted by adjectives that stay in one's mind.

Second and Third Readers: (taking the phrases turn about in quick succession) "They forsook the Lord," "and provoked him," "dealt proudly," "hardened their hearts," "did evil again," "trusted not," "murmured against," "sinned a great sin."

First Reader: At one time God told Moses:

Second Reader: "Say to the people of Israel, 'You are a stiff-necked people; if for a single moment I should go up among you, I would consume you'" (Exod. 33:5).

Third Reader: (after a pause) It makes you wonder what God thinks of us. We are so stiff-necked today.

First Reader: And so it went on. God sent his prophets to speak to them, saying, "Thus saith the Lord," but still their eyes strayed to other gods. Then God spoke to them through Isaiah, of a new kind of covenant.

Second Reader: Isa. 42:1-9

First Reader: The people yearned for this servant, for a Messiah, but it was many years before John the Baptist came crying, "Repent, for the kingdom of heaven is at hand" (Matt. 3:2). And many did humble themselves and repent, but the stiff-necked looked for a Messiah who would lead them to victory until their enemies were trampled underfoot.

Second Reader: But when Jesus came, he was not what they had expected at all. There came a night when he met with his disciples in an upper room.

Third Reader: Mark 14:22-25

First Reader: And then he was crucified.

Second Reader: But he rose again from the dead, and, as he had promised, the Holy Spirit came upon his disciples, and Peter addressed the people. Thousands repented and were baptized, and a new community came into being.

Third Reader: The high priest and his followers tried to stamp out the new teaching, and again God spoke—this time through Stephen, just before he was stoned to death.

First Reader: Acts 7:51-53

Second Reader: This time it was different. It was not the people who were "stiff-necked" but their religious leaders.

Third Reader: Slowly the church came into being. In Antioch, for the first time, the people of the church were called Christians. Then God made it clear that the Gentiles were to be accepted also.

First Reader: Acts 11:17-18

Second Reader: Already the church was changing, and went on changing. Sometimes for the worse, when its people were "stiff-necked," sometimes for the better when God forgave them and renewed his own.

Third Reader: Augustine prayed that the church might be forgiven for its sins, as it is here on earth not "without spot or wrinkle."

First Reader: Hundreds of years later Martin Luther described the pilgrimage of the church: "It is not yet done and accomplished, but it is going on. It is not the end, but the way. It is not all glistening and shining, but it is all being swept." [11]

Second Reader: Think about our beautiful churches scattered all across America. Their floors are not only well swept, they shine with wax.

Third Reader: (Interrupting) A well-waxed floor is a status symbol of the comfortable church, just as anointing the head with oil was a religious status symbol to the Hebrews.

Second Reader: But this is not what Luther was talking about. He was talking about the *people* who walk on the well-swept floors, the people who are the church, the church which is in constant need of renewal.

First Reader: "Be ye renewed" does not mean—"get busy and find some different and better method of Christian action." It means, "Expose yourself to the life-giving work of God. Pray that he may make the dry bones come to life. Expect great things from him. And get ready to do what he commands."

Second Reader: "This is a very practical truth. For it implies that the renewal of the church does not begin with more or less solemn decisions of synods, conferences or committees, but with an encounter between God and men, in which God takes hold of the situation and empowers them to serve as his instruments of renewal." [12]

Suggestions for Discussion and Action:

There is a restlessness in the churches of the world today. Something is lacking, but what? Some blame the leaders, some blame the people. There is no need to be like the woman who showed dissatisfaction with her church by deliberately singing off-key! We know we have become stiff-necked, but don't know what to do about it. Is your own group stiff-necked? Why not discuss this, even though it is easier to discuss the weaknesses of other groups?

What *should* your group be?

Recently, two youth associates on the staff of the Episcopal National Council returned from six months of field work related to young people. They commented: "There are four heresies in youth work." You might want to relate them to your group, and its place as part of your church.

"1. The 'future-church' heresy, dealing with young people as the churchmen of tomorrow.

"2. The 'numbers-game' heresy, measuring success in youth work by the number of young people who can be persuaded to be 'active' in one aspect or another of the total youth program.

"3. The 'street-cleaning' heresy, setting up programs to keep boys and girls off the street even though secular organizations as well as other churches are also ministering to the same young people.

"4. The 'stop-gap' heresy, involving young people in a variety of organizations which substitute busy work for solid nurture in the faith and preparation for mission in the world." [13]

After you have considered these questions, have someone read Jas. 4:8—"Draw near to God and he will draw near to you." Then with God's help and guidance, do something!

See Chapter IX for ideas, including some of those suggested by the Episcopal National Council in answer to the charge of heresy! See if your church has the magazine from which these ideas were taken.

1333707

Prayer:

Draw near to us, O God, and bless us. Give us grace to know thy will for those gathered here as a part of thy church, and give us the strength to do it. Amen.

6. A NEW CHURCH IN A NEW TOWN

Scripture: Matt. 5:14-15 ("A city set on a hill cannot be hid.")

Reading:

This is the story of a new church in a new town; of Kildrum Parish Church in the town of Cumbernauld. Kildrum means "the church on the hill" in Gaelic, the language of old Scotland. This town of Cumbernauld is an overflow from the city of Glasgow, one of the most depressed areas in Europe and constantly haunted by unemployment.

Cumbernauld did not grow from a store and a gas pump at a crossroads. It was planned—with housing all round the Town Center where multilevel shopping, parking, cultural centers, hotels, etc., are gathered together. No one will live more than twenty minutes from the Town Center. (In Scotland that can mean still twenty minutes on foot!) Schools, parks, and recreation facilities are strategically placed. And right in the middle, on a hill, stands the new church!

The people in this new church are mostly young families and they take an active part not only in the worship, fellowship, and prayer, but in the community in which they live. In fact, they must promise to do so when they become church members. They take part in the Tenant's Association, political parties, industrial and social groups—with Christian concern, and voicing their Christian convictions. For example, one group of women from the church look after the sick and old in the town, and a group of men paint their houses inside and out.

The church started in a hut in a wood, on a hill. In December, 1962, the completed buildings were dedicated, and the bells rang out from the new bell tower that can be seen from all parts of the town.

At this time a prayer was written for Cumbernauld:

"O God grant us a vision of our new town, fair as it might be: a town of righteousness where none shall wrong his neighbour; a town of plenty, where evil and poverty shall be done away; a town of brotherhood, where all success shall be founded on service, and honour shall be given to nobleness alone; a town of peace where order shall not rest on force, but on the love of all for the common life and weal. Bless the efforts of the Church to make the vision of living reality through the teaching of Thy Son, Jesus Christ. Inspire and strengthen each one of us, that we may give time, thought and sacrifice to speed the day of its coming beauty and righteousness; through Jesus Christ our Lord. Amen." [14]

Suggestions for Discussion and Action:

When you hear of a new church being built, you usually assume it will be in some modern style, and are familiar with articles and pictures of contemporary church architecture. Rarely do you see plans for the life of the new church.

Find out if there are any new churches (of any denomination) in your area, and go and visit them. If a floor plan seems unusual, find out why this is so and what function it serves. Try and discover what the life of this new church will be, in relation to the people who live near it, or will be its members.

Read I Cor. 12:27–13:13. Looking on this as a blueprint of the life of the people who will be the church, discuss the kind of church you would plan if you had the opportunity. Try to forget the usual building format and organization of the people, but remember that this will be the place where the people will come to worship God, receive the Sacraments, and relate both to everyday living.

Prayer:

Use the prayer that was written for Cumbernauld, changing the words to suit your town or community.

7. A CHURCH IN THE INNER CITY

Scripture: Matt. 5:16 ("Let your light so shine before men.")

Reading:

George W. Webber is one of the ministers of the East Harlem Protestant Parish, in the heart of New York City. Here Puerto Ricans, Negroes, and a few immigrant groups live in densely packed tenement buildings. Most of them feel utterly rejected by society, and feel that the church has rejected them too. How can they be shown the activity of Christians, and what their worship means? Here is one way:

"In a neighborhood where many people will never set foot inside the church and see no evidence of God in their world, it seems important that the church find dramatic ways of witnessing in public to his presence and activity.

"Our Easter Dawn service is an example of what we mean. At 6:30 in the morning the members, several hundred strong, gather on a big thoroughfare at the edge of a large public housing project. They begin with prayer and then proceed to march through the project singing the sad hymns of Good Friday a reminder of the way in which on the first Easter the women marched in sadness to the tomb. Halfway to the place of worship, the whole procession becomes silent. They arrive at the scene of the 'tomb,' a pile of rocks and a fallen cross in a public park, visible to the whole community. One of the ministers steps forward and in a loud voice announces, 'Christ is risen. This is Easter Day. Alleluia.' Everyone breaks into the Easter hymns. The service that follows is brief: sermon, prayers and hymn. Then the whole congregation marches back through the city streets and the projects, singing the joyful hymns of Easter, waking everybody up all over again, announcing that Christ has risen and Christians are shouting the good news to the whole world." [15]

Suggestions for Discussion and Action:

In what way is this congregation, and its worship, quite different from your own? (That is, if you are a member of a comfortable church.)

38

Could such a group gather outside your church—either for worship led by the pastor, or with your own youth group?

What would be the chief difficulty?

Is our brand of Christianity too reserved and inhibited? Do we tend to belittle those whose faith shows itself in simple exuberance, assuming that it goes with those who have less education and money? Where do we get the idea that Christ was respectable, and died only for the respectable?

Think about these words George F. MacLeod once wrote:

"I am recovering the claim that Jesus was not crucified in a cathedral between two candles, but on a cross between two thieves; on the town garbage heap; on a crossroads so cosmopolitan that they had to write his title in Hebrew and Latin and in Greek (or shall we say in English, in Bantu and Afrikaans); at the kind of place where cynics talk smut, and thieves curse, and soldiers gamble. Because that is where he died and that is what he died about. And that is where churchmen should be and what churchmanship should be about." [16]

You may answer, "But there are no people like this, where we live!" Maybe there are no Puerto Ricans and no slums, but are there no Negroes? No kids in trouble with the police, no unmarried mothers? Are there no conditions in your community that are a hardship on some minority? Is there no one on welfare? No one sick, penniless, or lonely? If there are people like this, what does your church say to them in action and in word? In what way do you *proclaim* your faith?

What action can you take? For example, what kind of "light" do you show at Easter or Christmas, as a congregation? Do you always have the same "programs" and services, for yourselves, or do they draw in those on the outside too? Are they always in the church building? Why?

Prayer:

O Lord, shake us out of our church habits, if they have lost their meaning, and give us an awareness of what they should reflect—not only to those around us, but to those who have never set foot in our church. Help us to know what to say and what to do. Amen.

8. THE CHARRED CROSS

Scripture: Eph. 4:31-32 ("Forgiving one another, as God in Christ forgave you.")

Reading:

It was not even a real cross. Along with a tall spire and some ragged broken walls, it was all that remained of a great cathedral. The morning after the air raid someone must have wandered in sorrow and anger among the rubble—perhaps a fire fighter, perhaps one of the clergy, or one of the people of the town. Whoever it was took two charred beams and tied them together with a bit of wire, in the form of a cross. Later, someone made a rough altar of fallen stones. There they both stood for over twenty years, with the words "Father Forgive" engraved on the wall behind them. They were symbols of the faith of a people who knew that, one day, the war would be over, and a new cathedral would rise again to the glory of God.

And it did! From this place, known as "the sanctuary of the ruins," you can look through the empty windows of the old building to the new Coventry Cathedral. You can look through the great wall of clear glass, engraved with the figures of saints and angels, and deep into the Cathedral itself. When you are inside, you can look out on "the sanctuary of the ruins" and the repaired town of Coventry. This was planned deliberately, so that the new Cathedral seems to say not only "Come in," but "Go ye out into all the world."

The charred cross was flown to the United States for the New York World's Fair. For many years it has been a symbol of reconciliation to all men, and many thousands will have seen it, remembering not only the German fire bombs that destroyed the Cathedral, but the words "Father Forgive." And there *was* forgiveness and reconciliation, for sixteen young German craftsmen asked for permission to help build the International Centre of Christian Reconciliation, within the ruins. Later the Cathedral choir gave concerts in Berlin to repay the young men who had helped them.

A charred cross. What does it say to us today of the place of the church in a war-weary world?

Suggestions for Discussion and Action:

Read the scripture again and II Cor. 5:16-19.

Try to have some of the many articles and pictures of Coventry Cathedral ready at the meeting. Your library may have a copy of *Phoenix at Coventry* by Sir Basil Spence,[17] the architect of the Cathedral. You may find pictures of the charred cross taken at the New York World's Fair.

Let everyone see these things, evidence of the great assembly of talent that goes into the making of a cathedral for the glory of God, even though much of it may be in a modern style which many still find hard to get used to. There has been criticism of the new Cathedral, but not of its symbol of reconciliation.

Reconciliation always sounds so easy! Can you think of some conflict near you where reconciliation is needed and see if you can do something to achieve it? Remember that we cannot direct people as if they were puppets, that we can neither judge nor take sides, and that prayer must be in the thick of it.

Perhaps there is a branch of the American Friends Service Committee in your area. If so, invite a speaker, hear of their work, and learn the Quaker approach to reconciliation.

See Chapter IX for information on the work of Coventry Cathedral in the community and its Youth Hostel.

Prayer:

Dear Heavenly Father, although the possibility of reconciliation between the powers of the world today seems all but impossible, we cannot forget that the decision and the real power is thine, O God, and with thee nothing is impossible. Grant that our prayer may be an avenue leading to peace, and direct our lives toward this end. In Jesus' name we pray. Amen.

9. WHAT IS THE SHAPE OF THE CHURCH FOR THE WORLD OF TOMORROW?

Scripture: Heb. 12:12-14 ("Strive for peace with all men.")

Reading:

"The congregation of the future will live under a common discipline. It will take seriously not just the "gathering," but the going forth. Think of the freedom such a congregation would have— its mobility, with almost none of the paraphenalia or baggage of the institution—with all its energy available for its mission.

"This is not to say that the past has nothing to contribute to the new shape. The experience of the past will be drawn upon more than it is at present. What I am describing is much more difficult than anything we have ever done. If anybody thinks this way is easier, he should find two or three people who really know what it means to be reconciled to one another and should inquire of them—people who are living out in their common life a prefiguration of what life ought to be in business, education, or medicine.

"Such Christians will not say, 'Come with me to church and maybe somebody there will be able to be the instrument of God's reconciliation.' They will say instead, 'You are now in church. We are right with you where you are. We will be the instrument of God's reconciliation to you here.' They will say, 'We are the church. We are that miracle of God's grace.' Of course this will not be said in just that way, but this is the conviction that will have to be expressed.

"The tendency at present is almost always to try to relocate the

42

people we would like to help. We say, 'If I can just get them to church, everything will be all right.'

"What we must learn to say is: 'Here we are. We are going to be with you right where you live. We're not going to pull you out of your environment; we're not going to make you a part of an institution to keep the institution going. And if we have to live with you in a tent for the rest of time and just witness to the fact that Jesus Christ, who is a servant, is at work in this world, we are going to make witness to that.' . . .

"Somebody says, 'Aren't you afraid of what this would do? Everything would go to pieces. Thousands of new congregations. Hundreds of new denominations.' Such a prospect doesn't worry me a bit, not one tiny bit. It is only a part of what I see as I try to discover the shape of the future. Maybe as you see what *you* see, and we get together under God, we will see something quite different from what either of us now sees. What is the shape to come? What is the shape of the church for the world of tomorrow?" [18]

Suggestions for Discussion and Action:

Gordon Cosby, who wrote the words you have just heard, was ordained as a Baptist minister and conceived the idea for the Church of the Saviour, Washington, D.C. It is probably more talked about than any church in America today, and its fame for such a totally different approach to the meaning of church membership has spread abroad. In 1958 Mr. Cosby and his wife were invited to attend the Ecumenical Institute of the World Council of Churches, in Switzerland. He spoke on the mission groups held in his church. (For a more complete account see "The Church of the Saviour, Washington, D.C.," pages 155-58.)

What do you think of his ideas? What would happen if we had no church institutions? (It may help you to evaluate their services and worth, before discussing this.)

Mr. Cosby also feels that we should consider giving up all professional ministries and that the church should not own real estate. What about these points? Do you know all the facets of the work of your minister and the type of training he has received? How does his job differ from that of the layman? You might, cautiously, invite your minister to discuss theses points with you!

Consider these words from the last paragraph of the reading. "Maybe as you see what *you* see, and we get together under God, we will see something quite different from what either of us now sees." How *do* you see the church of tomorrow? Before you decide—do you know the church of today well enough to be in a position to speak? Will this be the starting point of your action?

Prayer:

"Go forth into the world in peace; be of good courage; hold fast that which is good; render to no man evil for evil; strengthen the faint-hearted; support the weak; help the afflicted; honor all men; love and serve the Lord, rejoicing in the power of the Holy Spirit. The grace of the Lord Jesus Christ and the love of God and the fellowship of the Holy Spirit be with you all. Amen." [19]

ADDITIONAL WORSHIP RESOURCES

Scripture:

Ps. 127:1 ("Unless the Lord builds the house.")
John 4:1-24 ("Worship in spirit and truth.")
Acts 2:35-47 ("All who believed were together.")
       4:8-13 ("The head of the corner.")
       5:27-39 ("Gamaliel stood up.")
       6:1-7 ("Men . . . we may appoint to this duty.")
       10:34-48 ("The Holy Spirit fell . . . even on the Gentiles.")
       11:19-26 ("The disciples were for the first time called Christians.")

I Cor. 13:8-13 ("I gave up childish ways.")

14:40 ("All things should be done decently and in order.")

Eph. 1:3-23 ("Live for the praise of his glory.")

4:1-7, 11-16 ("Lead a life worthy of the calling.")

I Pet. 2:9-10 ("You are God's people.")

Prayers:

O God, forgive us for standing and watching your church, instead of remembering that we are called to be a part of it. We have sinned in seeing it as merely a product of the organization and prayers of men and women, down through the ages; instead of being the instrument of your Son, Jesus Christ, in the world yesterday, today, and tomorrow. Call us from our inattention and irresponsibility; strengthen and lead us. Permit us to be aware of your purpose for the church, now, and in the years to come; and grant us the privilege of taking an active part in it, through the Spirit of Christ. Amen.

O God, who in every age has called the young, the strong, and the eager to continue the life of the living church, take hold of us now, we pray; fill us with understanding and wisdom; give us daring and courage; give us love and humility; and send us out to serve the church in the world today, with the Spirit of Christ in our hearts. Amen.

"Thou who standest beyond both the darkness and the light, who art hidden by the names we give thee, and who movest in mystery to touch us to life, grant us in this hour the glory and power of thy presence. Break through the safe customs of our praise, turn back the thin devices of our devious fear, and let us hear thy word reverberate in the high places of our hearts and in the deep abysses of our need. If religion has protected us from thy mercy, or our prayers smothered our rebellion and sin, or our faith made thy grace futile, then put us straight, undeceive us, and bring us where we will find that thou art our Saviour and our Lord. Amen." [20]

Eternal God, we never cease to be amazed at the wonder and beauty of your world. Spring always comes, with the renewal of life in flower and leaf and bird. We cannot look at the sky or the sea, the mountains or wide plains, without thankful hearts; knowing that you are the creator of all things.

We thank you also for the works of men; for computers, refrigerators, X-ray equipment, skyscrapers and spaceships. These things all come from you as well, for you have created the men who made them.

We thank you for the church of today, where men and women may gather together to praise and worship you with hymn and prayer; where they may listen to your Word in the Bible and relate it to life with renewed vitality. Amen.

O Lord God, as we prepare to prune those branches of the church which have outlived their usefulness, let us not be so ruthless that we destroy the life-giving force within the church. Amen.

Hymns:

The Church's One Foundation
Jesus, with Thy Church Abide
Glorious Things of Thee Are Spoken
How Lovely Is Thy Dwelling Place
O Where Are Kings and Empires Now
Christ Is Made the Sure Foundation
Father of Men, in Whom Are One
O Word of God Incarnate
O Day of Rest and Gladness

For details on the use of worship resources, see the Introduction, pp. 17-18.

COME OUT, COME OUT, WHEREVER YOU ARE!

1. GLORY TO GOD IN THE HIGH ST.

Scripture: Rom. 15:1-7 ("Together you may with one voice glorify the God and Father of our Lord Jesus Christ.")

Reading:

The river Clyde runs through the city of Glasgow to meet the sea, and there are ships of all nations coming up and down it. It is not surprising that the men of Glasgow are ship builders, and that the banks of the Clyde are crisscrossed with the shapes of hulls and keels, gantries and scaffolding.

But shipbuilding is a fickle industry, and in the great Depression of the 1930's the Glasgow yards were silent, and its streets by the river were full of men standing in little groups. They were silent too, with the despair of the unemployed.

Standing in the heart of this district was Govan Parish Church —an ordinary church with pews and hymnbooks and the usual stained-glass window with a text engraved on it, saying, "Glory to God in the Highest." But it didn't say much to the unemployed men standing in the rain in the street outside. In fact, but for a faithful few who came to the services, people barely noticed that the church was there. Except, perhaps, for one small boy who threw a rock at the stained-glass window and neatly removed the "e" in "Highest."

The text now read, "Glory to God in the High St." The minister of the church, the Reverend George F. MacLeod, liked the change. To him, the word "glory" meant much more than part of a verse read at Christmas or sung in a carol. To him it meant the manifestation of God on earth, or, as Wycliffe translated it—"glorify" meant "to clarify," to make God clear to all men.

George MacLeod was becoming more and more convinced that the church should be working to glorify God, not only inside the building, but out in the "High St." (which would be main Street in America). To his regret, the window was repaired, but by then he was meeting at the street corners with the men. He had organized workshops where they made furniture. They soon knew they could get a bob (twenty-five cents) a day and a meal at Govan Church, and that this man cared enough for them to come out of his study and work and talk with them in the despairing streets, in the wind, and in the rain.

This, and other experiences, led him to the formation of the Iona Community, and the fulfillment of his dream that men should go out into the world, carrying the "Good News" of the whole church, of work and worship, politics and prayers, united to the "Glory of God in the Highest."

Suggestions for Discussion and Action:

Read the scripture again and II Cor. 2:14, noticing that word "everywhere."

In what way, do you think, did George MacLeod get to know these unemployed men? Would he have invited them into the church to sing a few hymns? You may be helped by the words in an article written by John MacMillan about this incident, "He taught and loved Govan and Govan loved and taught him."

What is happening outside your church building? It will be quite different, but can you find some situation where people are feeling alienated from the world around them? Perhaps a family with some problem, or a bewildered foreign student? Perhaps someone in your age-group who doesn't feel "good enough" to meet with you because he dropped out of school? There may even be a family on relief—would you know if there was?

Try to plan some direct or indirect action.

For further information on the Iona Community, see Chapter VII, pp. 176-78.

Prayer:

O Lord, shake us out of our comfort into an awareness of the misery that may be around us. Give us the mind of Christ to see people as they are, and not as conditions have made them. Help us to know what to say, and what to do. In Christ's name we pray. Amen.

2. THE GODFORSAKEN PEOPLE

Scripture: Luke 4:18-19 ("Proclaim release to the captives.")

Reading:

How many ships have crossed the Atlantic and entered New York harbor?

How many ships, battered by storms, and carrying far too many people huddled below deck, have come from Germany, Russia, Poland, England, Armenia, Ireland, Hungary, Greece, or Italy?

How many husbands and wives, children and grandparents, uncles and aunts have come, fleeing from the miseries of war, religious persecution, and famine? All of them waited for the moment when the cry would ring out:

49

"Land in sight!"

And then: "The Statue of Liberty!"

How many tens of thousands of people have rushed up thousands of decks to look at the great statue, symbol of the promised land to the weary immigrant?

How many Americans today, on the floating hotels that seem to be remote from the ocean they cross, will pause in their shuffleboard or six-course dinner to look at the Statue of Liberty with a surge of emotion and pride in their country?

They remember, while they were in school, learning the words inscribed on the statue. Maybe the weary and miserable who came in the battered old ships, knew them too—in several dozen languages.

> "Give me your tired, your poor,
> Your huddled masses yearning to breathe free,
> The wretched refuse of your teeming shore.
> Send these, the homeless, tempest-tost to me;
> I lift my lamp beside the golden door." [1]

For many of the immigrants the words were dreams come true. They surged through New York and out to the West and South, to scatter, settle, and leave little trace of their national backgrounds, except unpronounceable names and a few recipes.

But there were some to whom the words became a mockery, and the promised land the end of all hope. There were some who sank deeper in the bottom of New York, as the city lifted her buildings higher and higher in the air, pushing up proudly from the huddled masses at her feet.

America—the land of the free and the home of the brave. Only sometimes bravery was not enough. Physical strength and an opportunity were needed too.

Take the Irish. In 1847 nearly 53,000 of them staggered into New York, dying of starvation after the failure of the potato crop. Most of them were too weak to work. They brought typhoid and typhus, cholera and tuberculosis. They left one of the most beautiful countries in the world to crawl hopelessly into stinking cellars. The tremendous numbers, and the diseases the Irish brought, overwhelmed and frightened the Americans who offered generous help. They did what they could. Some were helped, but many died, and many more lived on with hate in their hearts. This is what happens when people lose hope. They trust no one. They break the law. They become a Godforsaken people.

It is over a hundred years since the Irish fled from famine, but the slums of New York are still filled. Today it is the Puerto Ricans, who fled from an equally lovely land to tenements where rats gnaw the feet of their babies; and they are stuck too, in hopeless misery. A Godforsaken people.

The Negroes come up from the South with the hope of equality, of better education, and opportunity for work, and they become a Godforsaken people too.

Who calls them Godforsaken? The clean and comfortable, pointing with a white-gloved finger.

You, in your smug suburbs with garbage disposal units, have you smelled any open drains lately?

You, with your automatic washer-and-dryer combinations, have you ever had to manage with one cold tap?

You, who "live better electrically," have you never, when temporarily inconvenienced by power shortage, wondered what it must be like to have no heat?

Perhaps these things, glimpsed—but not smelled—over TV or in the pages of a glossy magazine may move you to a surge of pity that says, "Let George—I mean the church—do something!"

What would your church do? If you painted and patched the derelict churches in the slums, would that kind of people want to come to your kind of church? Why should they?

Does God forsake his people? Did Christ forsake the poor, the sick, and the outcast? Hasn't it been the other way round? Hasn't God forsaken those who forsake people in need?

Could it be that God has forsaken not his people, but the organization known as the church?

Suggestions for Discussion and Action:

What do you feel the church should do? Admit it has failed in the slums and close the rest of the church buildings there? See if God is, perhaps, pointing to some new way of caring for his people, whom he does not forsake?

Recently, a booklet was published called *The City—God's Gift to the Church*. Strange title! What do you think it means? Here is a quotation from it; you may want to discuss it, along with the selected scripture:

"The city, by the very nature of the difficulties it presents, forces the churches which seek to witness in its midst to look for answers and new forms of Christian life which can be offered as gifts to the Church at large. God is speaking to the whole Church from the city streets as well as from other places of mission. God is giving gifts of witness and insight into the gospel which may be shared. Traffic runs two ways." [2]

If you feel you do not know enough about some of the signs of God's gift of the city, choose some of the topics related to it in this chapter for further study. If you live in or near a large city, find out if new and different things are happening there too, or check the names and addresses of parishes, industrial missions, etc., listed in Chapter IX, where you can get further information.

Prayer:

O Lord God, we give thanks for our homes and the comforts we enjoy. Forgive us that we so rarely notice the hardships of those who have little to be thankful for and have little to hope for. Draw us into some situation where we may see and know the ways in which you have led men from despair into hope again; through the knowledge of your son, Jesus Christ. Amen.

3. ARISE, GO TO NINEVEH—I MEAN CHICAGO

Scripture: Jonah 1:1-3, 3:1-9 ("Go to Nineveh, that great city.")

Reading:

The city is a restless thing like the sea. Its people surge in with the tide to work, and then back again at the end of the day to the suburbs—leaving those in the inner city like flotsam and jetsam on a beach at low tide.

Those who are left behind at the end of the day are the servants of the city. The janitors, busboys, street cleaners, waitresses, elevator operators, night clerks, and all the many unskilled workers whose occupations keep them there. There are also the unemployed, the drifters, the dropouts, the drug addicts, the street gangs, and thugs—the flotsam and jetsam of a city. Many are foreigners. Many are Negroes. Their numbers increase, and they have large families. As housing gets more difficult to find they move into areas that used to be middle-class areas, at the same time as the middle class is moving out into the suburbs.

Houses meant for one family are now crammed with ten. Property owners and realtors try to stem the tide by keeping rents high, but property values drop. This creates a problem for the city authorities as there is now less and less tax money available for education, fire departments, police, street maintenance, etc.

To add to the problem, there is an ever-increasing demand for bigger and better expressways to get the people to and from the suburbs and their work in the city. In the name of urban renewal this is being done. "Let's tear out those blocks of tenement houses. They should be condemned anyway, and we can build an expressway there." In the name of urban renewal this sounds good—but, people lived in those tenements! Where will they go? New housing is being built, but never enough to keep up with the tide of people, and so the blight of the slums spreads even farther out, with more and more people living in too small a space, with more and more anger and hate in their hearts.

What on earth has this got to do with the church?

Is there a possibility that God is saying to his church, "Arise, go to that great city! Go to Chicago, Detroit, Philadelphia, and New York"?

What do you think?

Suggestions for Discussion and Action:

Have someone prepared to give an outline of the Book of Jonah, or have the group study it now. Jonah was one of God's reluctant servants. (And there have been many of them!) He was called to do a job, and pretended he did not hear. He also relished the thought of the wicked being punished. (And there have been many like him!)

Discuss the relationship between our cities today and Nineveh. Is God calling his church or certain individuals to minister to his city?

The following viewpoints may help the discussion:

Gibson Winter has written two books on the problems of today's cities, both with provocative titles: *The Suburban Captivity of the Churches,* and *The New Creation as Metropolis.*[3] In the latter he expresses his belief that the church can no longer busy itself with its own religious buildings in a residential community, nor with the religious life of each individual member. He feels that a new "servant church" is needed, led by lay people who are qualified to understand the problems of the metropolis. This does not mean a new emphasis on urban problems, but a radically different organization in which the people of the suburbs begin to feel that they are responsible for the lives of the people in the slums, and *do something about it.*

Jane Jacobs has written a book called *The Death and Life of Great American Cities* [4] (which was condensed in the *Reader's Digest,* April, 1964, under the title, *The Right Way to Save Our Cities*). She agrees that cities are losing their middle-class populations to the suburbs, but feels that cities can grow their own middle class in the slums, with the right kind of help. She calls it "unslumming," and believes that if a metropolitan economy is working well, it will change many poor people into middle-class people, illiterates into skilled people, and help the mentally retarded to become more responsible.

The important thing is that the most successful should be induced to stay where they are, and this is not difficult as many of them want to do this anyhow. Miss Jacobs believes that most of the people of the slums are friendly and gregarious, and this helps combat the very real dangers of the inner city. Everyone knows what everyone else is doing. If they are scattered into new housing units, with longer blocks and too many open spaces and parks, not only are they unhappy, but there is an increase in crime.

These two writers present extreme viewpoints. In between are many interesting experiments (such as East Harlem Protestant Parish).

You might want to dramatize parts of the Book of Jonah, using contemporary situations with, perhaps, the main character fleeing to an easy, well-paying job, rather than the one he knows he should choose.

Prayer:

"Thou who movest in the dim beginnings, set before us the remembrance of saints and prophets, and of all the humble souls in whom the splendour of thy spirit shone through willing flesh and burning word, until at last we learn to walk in thy glory through the cluttered neighborhood of this imperfect world, doing thy will, even to the least of our brethren as unto thee, with praise and thanksgiving. Amen." [5]

4. "I AIN'T GOT NO USE FOR THE CHURCH!"

Scripture: I Cor. 1:26-28 ("God chose what is weak . . . to shame the strong.")

Reading:

The word "parish" comes from a Greek word meaning "district," and it refers to all the people living in an area under the care of a clergyman or priest, with their own church building. Most Protestant denominations look after what they call "their own" in a certain area, and leave the rest to find the way to "the church of their choice." They are punctillious about not asking a known Baptist to a Methodist service, and the whole situation becomes rather like the Masonic Order, where you may not ask a man to join; he must ask you, though you may throw out hints!

Among all those who have "their own church" is a vast number of people who could not care less; to whom the church means nothing, or even arouses dislike. These people are included under the term "parish."

We can learn from the Roman Catholics of the value of the parish system, and especially from Abbé G. Michonneau, who writes:

"Our parish is this entire territory; all those living in this section are committed to our care, without exception made because of nationality or immorality or hostility to the clergy. . . . Hence all those who do not come to us, and whom we will never get to know unless we go to them; all those whom we meet—including Algerians and Chinese—they are all our parishioners. . . .

"Our parish life should inform the life of all these people; . . . their workaday life; their life at home, at rest. That life is made up of the very air that they breathe, the things that occupy them, the joys and sorrows they have known, the influences which play upon them—the influence of the doctor who tends them, of the paper that interprets the world for them, of the leaders who direct them, of the public house at the street corner, of the theatre which sees them more often than the church does." [6]

The Abbé Michonneau's parish is in France, but the East Harlem Protestant Parish is in New York City. It is more like a colony, or a mission sent into the wilderness. Before it was organized in 1948 there was not a single Protestant church of a major denomination ministering with any effectiveness to the 250,000 people crammed into an area 30 blocks long and 7 blocks wide. This was the most congested area in the United States, with terrible housing, health, school, and sanitation problems.

The Parish began as a symbol of the concern of many Christians who felt the church was withering away where men and women needed it most. Eight denominations now work together to form this Parish: American Baptist; Congregational-Christian; Evangelical and Reformed; Evangelical United Brethren; Methodist; United Presbyterian in the U.S.A.; the Reformed Church in America; and the General Conference Mennonites.

When the young ministers of the Parish began calling, they met with rejection. "I ain't got no use for the church, and I ain't got no use for preachers," [7] was a typical reaction. The ministers realized that they must live with these people, share their problems, and get to know them. So they moved into tenements with their families and tried to listen, feel, and wait until they had, after several years, earned the right to minister to the people of East Harlem. And as they took part in God's gift of the city they found they themselves were ministered unto and inspired.

Someone is always being helped with the problems and tragedies of life, and discovering that the church cares about what happens to him.[8]

Suggestions for Discussion and Action:

Get permission from the city council or chamber of commerce in your community and (with those of other denominations if possible) take a religious census of several selected blocks. Plan beforehand how you can do this without antagonizing people, and yet try to find as much information as you can about the lives led, the church affiliations or lack of them. Then meet to discuss your findings in the light of the selected scripture.

Who are the strong, among the people you called on *and* among your own group? Those with the greatest faith, the greatest courage? Who are the weak?

If you wanted to get to know all these people better, how, in light of this particular situation, would you go about it?

Prayer:

O Lord God, as we try to know this group of people, keep us from the sin of merely being inquisitive, from the sin of being critical, from the sin of being self-righteous, and from the sin of being complacent. Give to us all the grace to accept one another with love and sincerity; through Christ who showed us the way. Amen.

5. GOD'S SWITCHBOARD OPERATORS

Scripture: I Cor. 12:4-8; 27-31 ("Varieties of service, but the same Lord.")

Reading:

This is happening in Portland, Oregon, and it would be hard to say who started it—nor does it matter who did. The thing that matters is the sudden surge of interest and ideas from many different groups, showing how God can be in a situation, stirring men and women to action in a dramatic fashion.

There is an area in Portland, down by the river, called Albina. Seventy-five percent of the Negroes of the city live here. No, the schools are not run-down and poorly equipped. They actually seem better than most of the schools for white students. Not only in buildings, equipment, teacher quality, curriculum, and methods, but in allowing field trips, more books, visual aids, and opportunities for initiative among the faculty and the students.

No, the streets are not dark and dirty. This is largely due to the "Alley Lady of Albina" (a worker for the Portland Development Commission), who organized the children to clear the debris and brambles from the back alleys, where rats were running. The children flocked to help her, for there were picnics and treats when the job was done. As part of the same project mercury-vapor lamps were installed, trees cleared to make room for them, and new ones planted by the residents.

This is not the whole picture. This merely sets the scene. The Negroes of the United States have been full of hope lately, as gradually and painfully their status improves, and more jobs are open to them. Unfortunately, with it comes the sickening realization that they do not have the qualifications for many of these jobs. Their education in the past was so poor that many adults are practically illiterate. Their children may have the best texts in school, but learning to read is like learning a foreign language, because an illiterate people do not use the language of books. Stories and pictures in the average school reader are planned for the middle-class families. There is no mention of rats, nor the deep sadness that Christmas can bring to the poor who cannot afford its gifts and treats. Jane and Billy in the readers, are white children. They never have to worry about whether or not there will be money to pay the doctor when they are sick. There is a family car, of course, books and toys, flowers, and the right clothes. Daddy always looks like a young executive, and the pretty lady baking in a modern kitchen is not a working Negro mother.

The schools are gradually changing their readers, but this takes time, and the need is *now!*

In Albina, some of the needs *are* being answered now.

A few students from Reed College offered free tutoring to pupils at Jefferson High who wanted to go to college or were apt to drop out. The idea was eagerly received by school officials and, as a result, hundreds of students from four colleges and some faculty wives as well, go to Jefferson High one night a week. The Portland School District provides a bus to get them there. They teach Spanish, Latin, math—anything that is needed—and adults come too, for tutoring in basic reading and math.

This is not all! Through the Greater Portland Council of Churches, married women who have been teachers are helping in the day time. Under the supervision of the school district, they either help the class teacher with groups in reading, music, sewing, and field trips, or give help after school hours. They send magazines and books home with the children, and encourage them to bring clothing that needs repair for other women to work on.

Behind these women (and a few men on their days off) are still more women who do baby-sitting, to release those needed in the schools, type, or make phone calls. Mrs. Charles Lutton, chairman of this group which includes eight denominations, once wrote to them:

"I have never beforehand understood so perfectly the Scripture that we are all members of the body of Christ. I hope you feel it too. It is so clearly evident in this work of ours—his teachers, his knitters, his secretaries, his drivers, his administrators. And I really feel like his switchboard operator, taking the calls, and putting each live wire in the right jack. I hope that whenever you see my name, you will know it represents you, and I earnestly hope that I will do this as he would have it."

Suggestions for Discussion and Action:

Read the scripture again, and discuss it in light of the last paragraph of the reading.

This account of what is happening in Albina is not merely an interesting story. Such things are happening all over the United States, each unfolding in its own way, and always the people of the church are working outside their buildings for anyone and everyone in need. Nor are they working on their own. In Albina school officials, social workers, college students, and many others besides those representing the church are achieving something together. It is not quite clear who started it, nor does it seem to matter, and it keeps going on. In the spring of 1964 those who were being helped are now helping! Students of Jefferson High organized recreation projects and interest clubs for those in the grade schools, and on a "buddy" basis they take younger children swimming and bowling. This resulted in pools and bowling alleys offering special rates and hours.

The question is, what can you do? Who will be your switchboard operator, and who the live wires?

Prayer:

Help us, O Lord, to find a situation where help is needed, and give us the opportunity to do something about it. Help us to work with others. Give us sensitivity and insight, especially where changes may have to be made; and above all, O Lord, constantly remind us that any publicity is to bring others in to help, rather than to throw the spotlight on us. Amen.

6. THE CASE OF THE CHURCH V. THE DEPARTMENT OF HOUSING

Scripture: Mark 3:3-12 ("His hand was healed.")

Reading:

When the church goes to work in the slums, living with the people, getting to know them, and understanding their hardships, it can sometimes do something to alleviate those hardships. If this is all, what is the difference between a church worker and a social worker? If this *is* all, there would be no difference.

Just as it is not enough for the church to talk about the love of God, and the forgiveness to be found in Christ, without doing something in life which is a reflection of this knowledge, so also it is not enough to live a life of love and service without saying why, without proclaiming the reason, or relating it to the reality of God.

Take as an example, the work of the church in East Harlem Protestant Parish.

Many of the landlords tried to save money by cutting down the heat. One very cold December the tenants of one building came to Don Benedict, a minister of the Parish at that time, to complain that they had had no heat for several days. He suggested they each get a thermometer and check the temperature in their rooms. After hearing the results, Don called the Department of Housing "and, before he could be shunted off to some other department, told the bureau that the tenants were all on welfare, would all certainly come down with pneumonia, and would cost New York a great deal of money if they didn't get an inspector up right away. . . . An inspector did come up that very day, and after taking a look at the thermometer readings, he set the thermostat at 80°. Shortly thereafter a summons was issued for the landlord to appear in court. It was a great day for the tenants when they and the minister together went to court to stand up before the judge and testify to the injustice to which they had been subjected. A kind of self-respect and integrity seemed to have been granted to them at last. However, on the way out of court one of the men said to Don, with real bitterness and considerable sadism, 'This is really terrific. We've got that old so and so over the barrel now. We're really going to make the landlord suffer.' . . .

"Now had been developed a relationship between the minister and this man which at least enabled them to talk at a new level of comradeship and understanding. In a direct way the man had poured the bitterness and hatred in his heart out where it could be seen." [9]

Suggestions for Discussion and Action:

With the comment of the man, "We're really going to make the landlord suffer," read the scripture again. Why do you think it was chosen?

Let's compare the paralyzed man with the people paralyzed by cold, for probably they all felt as bitter as the one who spoke up. Doesn't this show us where the church has the chance to play more than the part of a social worker? It must always be on the alert for an opportunity to preach—in this case about the sin of hate that can be bottled within us and of the healing which comes through the forgiveness of Jesus Christ.

It would have been easy for Don Benedict to have taken no notice of the man's remark. What kind of a conversation, do you think, took place between them?

Prayer:

Lord God, forgive us for the hatred and bitterness we so often keep bottled up in us, and especially for the cruel words we imagine we would like to say. No matter what is done to us, help us to remember that Jesus said, "Father, forgive them, for they know not what they do." Forgive us too, and help us to forgive others, through his name.

7. THE CHURCH IN THEIR HOUSE

Scripture: I Cor. 16:19 ("The church in their house.")

Reading:

John Henry Cardinal Newman once said, "Though the visible Churches of the Saints in the world seem rare, and scattered to and fro, like islands in the sea, they are in truth but the tops of the everlasting hills, high and vast and deeply-rooted, which a deluge covers." [10]

This could be a description of the "house churches" of today, scattered throughout many cities and seeming (at first glance) to have no relationship with an established church building. But the relationship is there, and must be, or the "house church" becomes just any neighborhood club.

What is this thing called a "house church"? It sounds new and yet is not, for people met in houses in New Testament days. At that time Christians were often banned from the synagogue, or they were a small group in a pagan town, perhaps meeting secretly. The idea of a special building came later. Since that time people have often met in a house, while waiting for a church to be built, but a "house church" is quite different. It is not temporary, and there can be many of them, connected *with* a church.

Ernest Southcott was one of the first to have this idea. A Church of England clergyman, his parish in Leeds was made up of a vast network of streets with row after row of small houses whose owners had small steady jobs in industry. Few had any interest in the church, but Canon Southcott asked some who did to invite their neighbors in for a chat round the fireside. They discussed any subject that came up, they had Bible study and prayer, and in particular, prayer for the needs of their neighbors on that street. Maybe they would finish with a cup of tea, and sometimes a Communion service would be held, round the kitchen table. The clergyman, or parish priest was always welcome, but did not have to be there (except for Communion).

Some of the people who came to the "house church" might not have been to a regular church for years, and some might never have been to one. When Communion was celebrated these people were invited to watch, and the clergyman might explain the meaning of the sacrament and what it meant to those who took part in it.

In a year as many as five hundred homes were opened to those who lived close by, and a new kind of friendship arose as they discussed their needs and the needs of the world, in the light of the Bible and with prayer. Instead of going to church, they were being the church.

There are house churches in this country, in Holland, Germany, India, and other parts of the British Isles. However scattered they may be, they are linked together under the surface as part of the church which is the body of Christ.

Suggestions for Discussion and Action:

When the church meets in a house, with those who live close by, it means that all ages are apt to be involved. In a church building the different age groups are usually segregated. Is this how it should be? (Try not to be influenced by what has been the custom.)

If a series of house churches were started in and around your neighborhood, would each of you want to take part in the discussions, in the intercessory prayers for neighbors, and inclusion of them at the meetings?

Tie your answers in with consideration of a recent idea that young adults have more opportunity to work with church leaders, and that a few of them should be asked to be deacons or deaconesses every year.

Prayer:

To the church of God in our town, and the people within it called to be followers of Christ Jesus, may grace and peace be given. Amen.

8. THE CHURCH AMONG THE CARROTS

Scripture: John 4:35-38 ("The fields are already white for harvest.")

Reading:

> Where is the church?
> Down among the carrots,
> Looking after babies, so the mothers can pick.
> Working in the cherries,
> Helping in the pears,
> Setting up a dance for the end of the day.
>
> Where is the church?
> Down among the lettuce,
> Teaching in a Bible school, off behind the barn.
> Working in the radishes,
> Helping in the strawberries,
> Fixing up a ball game, on a vacant road.
>
> Where is the church?
> Down among the apples,
> Loading up the pop machine for a weary crowd.
> Working in the string beans,

Helping in potatoes,
Handing out the hymnals, or leading in a prayer.

Where is the church?
Down among the celery,
Setting up a clothing sale, heating up the soup.
Working in the apricots,
Helping with tomatoes,
Handing out some medicine in a shabby shack.

Where is the church?
Down in the asparagus,
Talking with the growers, seeking steady jobs.
Seeing new machinery,
That will cut employment,
Facing automation, with bewildered migrant hands.

Where is the church?
Down among the sugar beets,
Helping migrants settle down, getting kids in school.
Teaching them some better skills,
Writing to the Congress,
Fighting to provide a place, for our fellow men.

Suggestions for Discussion and Action:

Read the scripture again.

It is easy to relate the life of the migrant workers to life in the Bible, for it tells of a wandering migrant people too. What is the big difference between the two ways of living?

Jesus uses these words to warn the people that the time of harvest is coming sooner than they think, and, of course, he is speaking of the harvest for eternal life.

We can interpret it in another way, as a warning to the migrants that a very different kind of harvest is coming, and is nearly here.

A harvest that will be gathered in without their help, for they will soon be replaced by mechanized equipment.

We are familiar with the work of the church among the migrants. The teaching and serving of these people in many ways, much of it on an undenominational basis and with many thousands of college students every summer.

What happens now? An all-out effort to help the migrants settle down and earn a living in some different way. Find out what is being done in your state. See if there is some way in which you can help. One million workers, and their families, need you.

Prayer:

Lord of the helpless people who work in the carrots; Lord of the wandering ones who pick the corn, and wander on to pick the apples; be with the undernourished children who play beside a field of beans; be with the older ones who pick the peas, but who should all be in school. Guard and protect them every one, as their chances of work grow less, and help them to find a place to stay at last. Amen.

ADDITIONAL WORSHIP RESOURCES

Scripture:

Rom. 16:1-5 ("The church in their house.")
Col. 4:5-6 ("Conduct yourself wisely toward outsiders.")
Rom. 5:6-8 ("We were . . . sinners, [yet] Christ died for us.")
I John 4:18-21 ("Love casts out fear.")
I Pet. 2:9-10 ("You are God's people.")
Matt. 10:29-33 ("You are of more value than many sparrows.")
II Cor. 2:14–3:3 ("The aroma of Christ . . . among those perishing.")
Matt. 11:2-6 ("Tell John . . . the poor have good news.")

Rom. 2:1-4 ("You have no excuse . . . when you judge another.")

Jas. 2:1-4 ("Show no partiality.")

Prayers:

O Lord, we are restless with some of the patterns of life that seem to have no meaning. If we meet change, help us to decide if it is for the better, and if it is, let us be ready to adjust to it. Amen.

O God, we thank you for the churches scattered throughout this great country of ours, where men are free to worship as they please. Forgive us that sometimes we forget this freedom and make our worship a trivial thing. As we gather here together, give us the strength to do the more difficult thing of taking the church out onto the freeway, the airstrip, through the mass mediums into the armed service, the factory, the school, and the business world, or wherever men may be. There, we know Christ will be waiting for us. Amen.

> *"Let us remember*
> that to become saints we have only
> to be what God wants us to be
> and to do what God wants us to do;
> to forget ourselves and never to forget God." [11]

O Lord, give us the appetite to be interested in all kinds of people and not only in our own crowd. Help us to learn to enjoy conversation with those who are older or younger, richer or poorer, of different color or nationality or different way of life. May we be alert enough to learn something from each contact with a stranger and add it to the store of our understanding of people, for they are all Thy people too. Amen.

Lord God, we live far from the inner city and have no opportunity to see the overcrowded slums, to know those who are actually hungry. Help us to read about them, talk about them, and find how their needs can be met. Give us the privilege of assisting those who work with them, through our prayers, now at this very moment. O Lord, be with them all, for the sake of thy son, Jesus Christ. Amen.

Hymns:

Lord, Speak to Me, That I May Speak
O Son of Man, Thou Madest Known
We Thank Thee, Lord, Thy Paths of Service Lead
In Christ There Is No East nor West
God of the Nations, Hear Our Call
Christ for the World We Sing
Where Cross the Crowded Ways of Life
The Light of God Is Falling
When Wilt Thou Save the People
Once to Every Man and Nation
Rise Up, O Men of God

chapter ‖‖‖

KEEP MY BROTHER?

1. SEEING THE UNSEEN

Scripture: Matt. 13:15-17 ("This people's heart has grown dull.")

Reading:

"This appeal is addressed to those who have eyes but do not see, to those who have ears but do not hear. It is a plea that eyes be used for seeing, ears for hearing. It is a petition that feet be used for walking so that eyes may see and ears hear. It is voiced in the hope that the comfortable will make the moral effort required to walk, see and hear before it is too late.

"Yesterday it was the Negro who was the invisible man in America. Like the blue-clad scene-changer in a Chinese play, he moved in and out and did his expected work, but he was supposed to be invisible, and for many Americans he was invisible. But one day in Montgomery, Alabama, invisible Rosa Parks refused to move to a back seat in a bus, and suddenly this little seamstress was a resolute, highly visible human being. Moreover, her visibility was contagious; with the help of Martin Luther King, Jr., and other

70

previously invisible people it spread until many of America's 20 million Negroes, who had been there all the time, emerged into awesome reality.

"Today the American poor are invisible, but signs multiply that they too are moving swiftly into view. . . . They say that multitudes of these persons are moving restlessly from worked-out mining regions and industrialized farms to the cities, where great numbers are already crowded into teeming slums long ago abandoned by all the "right people." Most incredible of all, they contend that these persons continue to love their children and to seek a better life for them, that they are dissatisfied with their role of invisible scene-shifters and intend to assume visible and speaking parts in the drama of American life. . . .

"We cannot reach the poor educationally or economically or in any other way until we learn to see and hear them. We cannot see and hear them until we stand in the presence of one or more of them, talk with them, sense something of the emotional strain from which they are never free. Until we lower the barriers which are so easy for the comfortable to raise and to justify, we dehumanize ourselves and our brothers. . . .

"Governmental action will amount to nothing unless we act through the churches to renew and strengthen an attitude of simple humanity. Simple humanity is not sentimentality, nor is it an emotional substitute for justice. It is the attitude of the good man who sees and hears his neighbor's need. It is Christian love personally reaching out not only to church members but to other persons in the community. It is the opposite of an all too prevalent current attitude which preaches hatred and urges its use to gain social justice or racial equality. Above all, it is the will to walk into face-to-face relationship with persons in need, even though they were previously invisible and unheard." [1]

Suggestions for Discussion and Action:

Michael Hamilton, who ministers to South mountaineers in Cincinnati, has said, "In order to minister to people you have to come down or up to where they are, not to get shocked or surprised at what they are or do, but to start with them from where they are, and not where you might like them to be. *God did not shout down advice to us humans over the ramparts of heaven, but rather came down and shared our problems.*" [2]

Discuss this quotation, and the reading, in light of the chosen scripture.

What can you do, not "for," but "alongside" persons in need? Chapter II, topic 5 ("God's Switchboard Operators"), may give you some ideas.

Prayer:

Lord God, in our hearts we have been dimly aware that many were not as comfortable as we are. We have made the mistake of feeling that this must be either their own fault or none of our concern. We have been blind to the plight of others; help us to see. We have been deaf to tales of poverty in our own country; help us to wake up and listen. Instill in us a sense of responsibility for our fellow men, so that we seek them out and discover what is happening. Under thy guidance, may we be granted the privilege of doing something for them and with them. In thy name we pray. Amen.

2. WE NEED A "GOOD SAMARITAN" LAW!

Scripture: Luke 10:29-37 ("The Good Samaritan.")

Reading:

George W. Webber, one of the ministers in East Harlem Protestant Parish, has likened the work there to a colony—God's colony. He has written:

"It was the task of the colony to offer with no strings attached the love of Christ, to care about the daily crises which made life chaotic and frustrating. In every possible way, the church sought to be the Good Samaritan. Many, perhaps most, of the people they served never have become church members, but somehow this was a place where you offered your help simply because these were people whom Christ loved and for whom he had died.

"But the parable of the Good Samaritan was often not directly relevant to many of the crucial social issues in East Harlem. One of the Parish ministers was walking down a street when he saw an old man struck down by a coal truck that was trying to beat the signal lights. The minister's first impulse was to pick up the bleeding man, put him in his car and take him to the nearest hospital. But the laws of our society make such action illegal. One cannot touch an injured person. The only thing for the minister to do, then, was to call an ambulance, meanwhile making the victim as comfortable as possible and holding back the crowd. It took an hour and thirty-seven minutes for the ambulance to arrive. The man died on the way to the hospital.

"The young colonist, wanting to be a Good Samaritan felt utterly helpless. Gradually the Parish came to understand that in its ministry to the world in Christ's name, it had to get involved in better ambulance service for the slums. This meant a specialized knowledge of political structures, a good deal of sustained effort and participation by a substantial number of concerned citizens. The answer, in other words, would have to lie in politics, in putting the kind of pressure on City Hall that would result in genuine relief for East Harlem. Only in such a way could any real effort be made to bind up the wounds of so many people in East Harlem. This has been a slow process, for political involvements are always ambiguous and frequently we find ourselves struggling against insuperable odds. . . .

"Our ministry to the world needs realism and relevance. It had to go beyond simply binding up the wounds of the victims of injustice. . . . In East Harlem it came to seem almost blasphemous to pray for the health of Marie who has caught tuberculosis in a rotting tenement, while doing nothing about the same rotting tenement where other little Maries would catch the same disease. A condition of church membership became a commitment for each member to participate actively in at least one community organization that was expressing social concern. . . . It was as important to work for the local PTA as to be a good Sunday School teacher." [3]

Suggestions for Discussion and Action:

Can you think of any situations in your community where it is difficult to help someone in need? Sometimes there are valid reasons why you should not (such as moving an injured person when you do not know the extent of the injury, or have had no training in first aid).

Even more difficulties present themselves when a doctor comes upon the scene of an accident. Naturally, he wishes to help, but in doing so he runs the risk of a lawsuit should the injured, or his family, decide his treatment was inadequate.

In many states doctors are cautioned by their medical association that it is unwise of them to stop, and unwise to carry anything on their car that will identify them as being doctors. At the same time the medical profession is trying, in many states, to push legislation that will protect them and free them to offer the help they want to give. There are now thirty states with a "Good Samaritan" Law. What would be the objections to such a law?

After discussion, it will be obvious that these problems are much more involved than they were in the days of the New Testament! Ask a doctor and a lawyer from your own church to give you information on the situation in your community and state.

Prayer:

Lord God, give courage to those who see that new or different laws are needed to protect everyone injured, sick, or exposed to exploitation. And whatever we can do, give us the chance to do it, even though public opinion may be against us. We pray in the name of Jesus Christ who first showed us how to be Good Samaritans. Amen.

3. A CUP OF COLD WATER

Scripture: Rom. 10:12-13 ("There is no distinction between Jew and Greek.")

Reading:

"Some years ago an elderly Englishwoman was visiting New Orleans. At that time there was no racial problem in England. She was dimly aware of two types of Negroes—one represented by the son of an African chief who attended Oxford University and was sought after by many hostesses as being 'so interesting'; and the faithful Aunt Jemima or Uncle Remus type, servants in a separate world of their own, who would never presume to enter hers, nor would she contemplate entering theirs. Visiting New Orleans, with its overwhelming majority of Negroes, brought a new experience as she boarded a street car and sat down in the nearest vacant seat.

"For a few moments a Negro woman across the aisle stared at her in amazement, then she leaned forward and said, 'You're sitting in the wrong section, ma'am.'

"The Englishwoman looked about her hastily, saw the sign 'colored,' and realized the white people were all sitting in another part of the street car, but she smiled graciously and said, 'That's quite all right, I don't mind.'

" 'You're not *allowed* to sit in this section,' said the other woman, with great dignity.

"In that moment the Englishwoman saw the Negroes as people for the first time, saw their pride, and realized that instead of having a desire to join the white people, they wanted to have equal opportunity as human beings. The white lady was so ashamed of her gracious condescension that she got off the street car at once.

"Without a startling incident like this, it is sometimes hard for those of one race to recognize those of another as human beings like themselves. There is little feeling of recognition when they look superficially at features and pigment of skin, so different from their own, while added to this there is often the further barrier of a different language and culture.

"All peoples are inclined to believe that their customs and traditions are the best and the right ones. Many white people carry this even further by assuming that other races have a burning desire to adopt *their* way of life! (In some ways this is understandable, as the white people have been largely responsible for better education, health, and industry in many of the more primitive parts of the world.)

"Here is an example of this zeal to implant customs in a foreign field. During World War II millions of Americans were sent overseas. Wherever they went they insisted on a glass of water with ice in it at their meals, assuming that not only was this correct, but that all non-Americans would gratefully drink iced water from then on. A trivial matter, and yet it is the multiplicity of seemingly trivial things that can lead to resentment.

"There are still many Christians who believe in world brotherhood, who hold services in February every year, emphasizing it with suitable Scripture and prayer, but who, through no fault of their own, can only pay it lip service, as they have not had the opportunity to live it. Therefore, they have no idea how they would act in a mixed racial setting.

"What can these sincere, honest people do about it? They can try to prepare themselves beforehand by becoming aware of interracial difficulties, and by remembering that it is God who creates the different races and man who erects the barriers between them.

"No matter where you live, and no matter what your experience has been so far, the chances are that some day you will travel: as a member of the armed services, or the Peace Corps; as a foreign exchange student; or as a happy tourist with a guide book and camera. Paul called himself an ambassador. What kind of an ambassador will you be? If you drink a cup of cold water with a brother of another race, will you insist that it be iced, and that he must agree his should be iced too? [4]

Suggestions for Discussion and Action:

The relationship between the chosen scripture and this topic is simple and obvious, but have you translated it into modern terms?

How many foreign exchange students or teachers have been invited to your group? Did they come as "guest speakers," separated from all of you, or were they in your homes as friends with whom you could exchange ideas? What more can you add to what you may have done already?

Prayer:

Deepen, O Lord, our understanding of the ways and needs of others. Amen.

4. AN EXTRA PAIR OF JEANS

Scripture: II Cor. 9:6-8 ("God is able to provide you with every blessing.")

Reading:

The following dramatic sketch should be played on tape, or over a public address system, as no visible action is needed.)

Joanne: Just look at this dreamy skirt! I hate to say it, but isn't this too *good* to send overseas? It's even the right length, and I'm sure the women in Peru don't know what is being worn in Paris.

Sue: What makes you so sure these clothes are going to Peru?

Joanne: Oh, I don't know. Wasn't it in the news lately? Some kind of catastrophe. I forget what.

Pat: Church World Service sends clothes all over the world, Joanne, to keep people warm.

Joanne: Good grief! Here's a shirt with a hole in the sleeve! We can't send that.

Sue: Why don't you patch it? We're supposed to be the Patch and Pack group. It wouldn't take long.

Joanne: But I didn't know I was meant to *work*. No one told me.

Pat: Oh, come on, Joanne!

Joanne: But I don't know who wore it, and it may not even be clean! I'll go and get a coke. Maybe do it when I come back. (exit)

Sue: That girl makes me so mad.

Pat: Her? Oh, she'll catch on one of these days. Something else bothers me.

Sue: Like what?

Pat: We give this stuff to be sent overseas, but really we're not giving anything at all!

Sue: I don't get you.

Pat: Well, most of it was just dumped here by people cleaning out their closets, and yet they all act as if they'd done a good deed. It makes me sick!

(enter Mike)

Mike: Got some more ready to go, Pat. And what's making you sick?

Pat: Oh, the way everyone gives themselves brownie points for giving away what they don't want, anyway.

Mike: Thing I notice is that they're all what you'd call "best" clothes, or things that go out of style. No warm work clothes. No blue jeans.

Sue: Guess the blue jeans always get worn out, and so there never are any to give away.

Pat: Sue, you've just had a neat idea!

Sue: I have?

Pat: Blue jeans! Let's ask everyone in our crowd to buy one *new* pair of jeans and include them. Then we'd be giving too!

Mike: You can sign me up for a pair!

Sue: Me too! Here's Joanne, we'll ask her.

(enter Joanne)

Joanne: Are we about through? I really should be going now.

Pat: Joanne, we've decided to ask all the kids who are in on this to give a brand new pair of jeans, to go with the consignment. How about you?

Joanne: Pat, you *know* I never wear jeans! 'Bye all. Been quite a workout, hasn't it?

(exit Joanne)

Mike: Well, how d'you like that!

Pat: Oh, never mind her. Let's go tell everyone else!

(exeunt)

Suggestions for Discussion and Action:

Plan some participation in Church World Service, or some other relief organization.

Prayer:

O Lord God, we know that much has been given us, help us to know that much will be required of us also. Amen.

5. KEEP MY BROTHER? WHO IS HE?

Scripture: Gen. 4:1-9 ("Am I my brother's keeper?")

Reading:

The words, "Am I my brother's keeper?" are constantly quoted by many people without much awareness of their context. This primitive story from the Old Testament leaves one with a feeling of sympathy for Cain! It did seem that God had discriminated against him. On the other hand, his answer was not very wise. In fact we could call Cain the first "smart Alec."

There are many interpretations of this story, but they refer more to disobedience and murder than brotherhood. The following reading from Deuteronomy tells much more.

(Read Deut. 15:7-11.)

"The poor will never cease out of the land." Jesus echoed these words many years later, when he said, "You always have the poor with you" (Matt. 26:11). Isn't it about time we acknowledged this fact, rather than trying to pretend the poor are not there and sweep them under the rug? If we do, then we must accept the fact that they are our responsibilities, they are our brothers. Too often we give to the poor merely to ease our own consciences. Such giving is like lagniappe—a little extra thrown in that you are not really required to give. This is wrong. We are told, "You shall open your hand to . . . [your poor brother], and lend him sufficient for his need, *whatever* it may be."

Perhaps, our failure to cope with poverty and hunger in the world today is due to our inability to keep up to date with the Old Testament! And when we say Old Testament, we mean God's Word to us through the Old Testament, which is still fresh today.

The trouble is, our poor brother is often so far away, and we comfortable ones do not know how to help him.

East Harlem Protestant Parish is well aware of this. George W. Webber writes, "In order to teach the little children that Christmas is giving as well as receiving, the Sunday school has a white gift offering. After a lovely pile of gifts has been presented (I am afraid sometimes purchased on Saturday afternoon by mama and dutifully wrapped up in a way that hardly gets across to junior the principles involved), someone says, 'My goodness, what shall we do with them now?' Apparently some Protestant churches are not even sufficiently in touch with their community to know where they can best be used. At that point someone remembers having heard of the East Harlem Protestant Parish and sends the gifts off to us." [5]

What do they do with them? Unwrap the white tissue paper, spread all the gifts out, and have a toy sale in the church, to which everyone is welcome to come and buy for their children, at a penny, a nickle, or a dime!

Perhaps the poor are better at helping the poor than we are! Here is a very different example of brother helping brother.

The island of Foula lies twenty-five miles off the Shetland Isles, over a hundred miles north of Scotland. It is one of the wildest places in the world, surrounded by stormy seas, and often cut off from the Shetlands for months during the winter. Its people are very poor, but are also brave, independent, and generous. In the summer of 1963 they gave $182.00 to the Freedom From Hunger Campaign. This represented $3.50 a head, and was *the highest contribution from any community in Britain*. The money was used to help reclaim land from the sea in South Korea—a project, run by the church, which will provide 1,500 acres of land for rice-growing. It is being done by over 1,000 refugee families who are lifting thousands of tons of dirt and rock to make a dyke more than a mile long and fourteen feet high.

Who is my brother? *We* don't seem to know much about him, do we?

Suggestions for Discussion and Action:

Ask for a definition of the word "brother" or "brotherhood," from your group (not as a blood-relation, but in the wider meaning). Don't forget that the word "fraternity" comes from the Latin *frater* (brother), and should be included too.

Too often, the word "brother" can just become synonymous for the word "man," and lose all meaning, or, when referring to lodges, unions, and fraternities it can become exclusive and discriminatory. Is either of these the correct biblical interpretation of the word?

Discuss some of the great difficulties of being "brotherly" today. What has caused them? What could you do at Christmastime that would have more reality than the white gift project?

Try closing with the hymn, "O Brother Man, Fold to Thy Heart Thy Brother." Read it aloud first. The opening line may sound very corny to us, but it was the accepted language of a poet of the nineteenth century, John Greenleaf Whittier. Remember, instead, when you sing it, the idea he was trying to convey, and that he devoted his life to the abolition of slavery.

Prayer:

Give to us, O Lord, a fresh understanding of words with which we have been familiar for a long time. Help us to remember that our "brother" is anyone we meet and anyone in need of help. Amen.

6. THE CHURCH IS FOR ANYBODY

Scripture: Matt. 25:34-40 ("I was a stranger and you welcomed me.")

Reading:

This is the story of Christ Church, Milwaukee. It is a Presbyterian church of the inner city that overflows with activity all week long, and from it can be heard the thump of a basketball, the whir of a sewing machine, and the cool notes of a hot band in the basement.

The pastor, the Reverend Robert E. Ryland, says "an inner-city church like this must be sensitive to the needs of people in the community. Whatever we do must be done not as 'bait' to get folks into church but out of genuine interest, reflecting Christ's concern for them." [6]

Such a simple aim, and one that every church member would go along with—but few carry out. Too many feel they are slipping up on their job if every contact with new people does not include a prayer, a little evangelism, and a promise to come to church next Sunday.

This old church had been flourishing in its day, but was down to forty-three members when Bob Ryland took over and when Mary Scott was hired as parish worker. She soon found that "the only way to win a really friendly rapport was to sit down and talk about the children's troubles in school or the tenant next door who persisted in doing her laundry at all hours of the night or the difficulties of resettling in a strange city.

"The needs that came to light were wholly unpretentious. But they were quite enough to trigger a chain of equally unpretentious new programs for the church: a drop-in supper for children with sparse opportunity for family meals around table, a learner's class in sewing for mothers, a story hour, an adult self-help program, and homework hours for children. . . ."

"Today as many as one hundred children show up on alternate Wednesdays for a family-style round-the-table drop-in supper, each child paying twenty-five cents if he has it. 'Table parents' from other churches exert the same kind of gentle authority they would at home: 'Elbows off the table, please,' or 'If you want something, ask for it.' After dinner, a sort of junior-grade amateur hour gives youngsters a chance to display their abilities. Recently, after several of the girls attended a Y.W.C.A. discussion downtown, one of them told Mrs. Scott, 'Our girls are different from the others. They know how to behave.' . . .

" 'The church has the message that everybody is somebody,' says Bob Ryland. . . . What most non-urbanites fail to realize, he continues, is that people in the city 'know they are born to live in a dump. Thousands never expect their lives to be any different.

" 'Anything that enables them to inch their way up a little is important. The most tremendous thing we can do is to convey the idea of human dignity—that it is God who, out of his love, wants them to develop.' " [7]

One hundred and fifty-nine people have volunteered to help with all these things, and many of them come from other Presbyterian churches in the area, anxious for the opportunity to take part in such an exciting venture. In the spring of 1963, there was talk of a romper room for preschool children to have a place to play; trips for teenagers to stimulate their cultural interests; luncheons with Negro intellectuals or non-Protestants; and discussion of the relation of the Christian faith to the world.

"Whatever new ideas get in the works, they won't be dull." [8]
It would be interesting to know what they are doing now!

Suggestions for Discussion and Action:

How much is your church used, on Sunday, and during the week?

Are there facilities that could be used for activities not directly connected with meetings, Sunday school, etc., both indoors and out?

What are the biggest needs in your community?

Can your church take care of any of these needs?

Bob Ryland has said, "We'll try anything that represents a need. If it is not needed, we drop it."

Can you come up with some ideas, and see if your minister and church leaders would let you try them out?

Examples: play school on Saturday mornings, or hobby clubs for older children; practice place for small music combinations; youth employment service headquarters.

Prayer:

Dear Lord, grant us ideas for serving the needs of others, but let us not fall into the error of filling the church with mere busy work. Let our church be full of sound and activity to the glory of thy name, although it may become untidy and tracked with the marks of many feet. Let its doors and windows be open wide to all sorts of people, rather than being shut, the church swept clean and empty. Amen.

ADDITIONAL WORSHIP RESOURCES

Scripture:

II Cor. 8:1-15 ("Your abundance . . . should supply their want.")

Matt. 22:36-40 ("Which is the great commandment?")
I John 2:7-11 ("He who loves his brother abides in the light.")
    3:17-22 ("If anyone has the world's goods and . . .
       closes his heart, how does God's love abide
       in him?")
    4:7-11 ("Let us love one another.")
Matt. 5:43-48 ("Love your enemies.")
I Cor. 12:12-26 ("If one member suffers, all suffer.")
Gal. 6:1-4 ("Bear one another's burdens.")
Rom. 12:9-19 ("Outdo one another in showing honor.")
Col. 3:8-15 ("Forbearing one another.")

Prayers:

"Lord God, . . . we pray for grace to give well, to help without patronizing, to assist without weakening, to share without diminishing the self-respect of others. Amen." [9]

"God, grant me the serenity to accept those things which I cannot change, the courage to change the things I can, and the wisdom to know the difference." [10]

"Almighty God, let no man seek his own good and forget his neighbor's advantage. Amen." [11]

Dear Heavenly Father, forgive us that we are so quick to be aware of the surface differences between ourselves and others. Help us to find the deeper qualities we share as members of the human race whom thou hast created and for whom Christ died; in his name we pray. Amen.

Hymns:

Rise Up, O Men of God
In Christ There Is No East or West
God of the Nations, Hear Our Call

Christ for the World We Sing
Where Cross the Crowded Ways of Life
O Brother Man, Fold to Thy Heart Thy Brother
Thy Kingdom Come, O Lord
At Length There Dawns the Glorious Day

chapter IV

NO MAN IS INNOCENT OF HATE

1. WHAT IS HATE?

Scripture: Luke 23:32-34 ("Father, forgive them; for they know not what they do.")

Reading:

> Hate is a seed,
> Born of distrust,
> Nourished with fear,
> Fanned by unfairness
> And urged by an anger that burns.
>
> Maybe a scowl,
> Words of disdain,
> A parcel of lies,
> Or a slap in the face
> That leads to an itch to kill.

Some call it just; some call it vengeance;
Some dare to shout that God's on their side.
            Bomb Hiroshima!
            Sneer at the Jew!
            Hose down the nigger!
            Kill children in church!
            And laugh when a president dies!

Once it began, when joy in a manger,
Was quenched by the death of innocent babes.
Slowly the spite and the spleen came closer,
Close, till the Christ was nailed to a cross.
Christ gave the answer, long since unheeded,
"Father, forgive, they know not what they do."

Suggestions for Discussion and Action:

Read Matt. 2:1-16, concentrating not on the familiar story of the nativity, but on the character of Herod the king. First he is troubled. Then he plots in secret, and his plot fails. In a furious rage, he orders the death of all the male children in Bethlehem under two years of age. Under it all you can see that "uneasy lies the head that wears a crown."

Dorothy Sayers said that Herod "was crafty, false, and suspicious, and had a vile temper; but he was a genius in his way. Caesar knew that Herod was the one man who could be trusted to keep Judaea in order. . . . Thus his being 'troubled' by the threat of a Jewish Messiah, and steps he took to suppress the menace were, from the political point of view, perfectly well justified." [1] Here you see another side of the picture. Add to this the fact that Herod had an inferiority complex because the strict Jews despised him as a descendent of the House of Esau, and not the House of Jacob, and you have a good example, though somewhat bloodthirsty, of the complex nature of all men, including ourselves.

You may want to discuss the complex nature of man, and the different situations that can lead to feelings of hate. Try and think of live examples in your own community, church, or group. Try to understand them, as you hope *your* expressions of hate will be understood and forgiven!

If you want to try to enter into the hate feelings that can be generated in a mob of people, act out a few of the crowd scenes in Dorothy Sayers series of plays, *The Man Born to Be King*. These plays caused great controversy when first performed over the British Broadcasting Company's radio programs in 1941 and 1942. This was during World War II, when feelings of hate were familiar, and Miss Sayers insisted that the plays be written in modern speech, which added greatly to the realism of these scenes written on the life of Christ. (Do not attempt to act the scenes in front of an audience, they are written for radio only, and can be relayed through a public address system, played on tape, or read aloud by a group.)

Prayer:

Forgive us, O Lord, for the hate feelings within us. Forgive us for the envy and bitterness, the distrust and the feelings of inadequacy that can cause us to lose all sense of proportion and value. Help us to remember that when such things are shared with others, they can become like a grass fire blown by the wind and destroy many things. Give us the insight to be aware of this weakness in all men and to avoid the temptation to point with the finger of criticism. We pray in the name of Christ, who taught us how to forgive one another. Amen.

2. AFTERMATH OF AN ASSASSINATION

Scripture: Matt. 27:20-26 ("I am innocent of this man's blood.")

Reading:

This reading is taken from a sermon preached in Dallas by the Reverend William A. Holmes on the Sunday after the assassination of President Kennedy.

"President John Kennedy was killed two days ago in Dallas, and the one thing worse than this is that the citizens of Dallas should declare unto the world: 'We take no responsibility for the death of this man.' Yet already that seems to be the slogan of our city and of some of its officials: 'Dallas is a friendly city—this was the work of one madman and extremist.' . . . 'Our hearts are saddened—but our hands are clean.' How neat and simple this solution! How desperately we wish that it were true. . . .

"There is no way in all creation to avoid our corporate and mutual guilt. By our timidity we have encouraged the aggressor; by our paralysis we have given safe-conduct to reactionaries; by our confusion we have promoted the clarity of evil; by our small prejudices and little hates we have prepared the way for monstrous and demonic acts that have betrayed us all. We have become a garbled people, mistaking patriotic cries for patriotism, boistrous boasts for courage, superficial piety for faith. In this week of blood-stained history and death we are under an imperative to whisper unto one another and to God: 'O Lord, have mercy on us all.'

"Yet there still hang the questions: 'What are we to be?' 'What are we to do?' By the grace of God, this much is clear. We are called to be a city where political debate continues. Different points of view must be expressed. . . . But the context of that debate in Dallas—as across our land—must be the context of mutual forbearance and good will. We must be as jealous of another person's right to think and live as we are jealous of that right for ourselves. It is not too late for us to learn that men can agree to disagree in love and still hold partisan persuasions. . . .

"John Kennedy is dead—killed two days ago in our own city. If Dallas, Texas, rises from this monstrous moment in her history, a new city where different political opinions and the people who hold them are respected, then John Kennedy will not have died in vain. But that remains to be seen. Until then, the one thing worse than his assassination in our midst is that we the citizens of Dallas should wash our hands and say: 'We take no responsibility for this man's death.' " [2]

Suggestions for Discussion and Action:

Read the scripture again. Discuss the many times and places when people say, "Well, I wash my hands of the whole affair!" Perhaps this comment can sometimes be made with good reason, but when it is not, what weaknesses does it usually suggest?

How much do we involve ourselves to the point of taking a stand on a controversial issue? How often do we say, "This is what I think, but don't quote me"? How often do we consider the teachings of Christ when we take a stand? How do we choose our political leaders? By good looks, cultural background, money, glamor, savoir faire, courage, a cosmopolitan aura we envy? (Yes, that is meant to be a description of the late President and his wife!) Or do we stand through a knowledge of the issues John Kennedy himself stood for?

How willing are we to take risks for our beliefs? (And what social-political beliefs should emerge as the result of Christian beliefs?)

When you don't "wash your hands of the whole affair," whatever it may be, you take a risk. Kennedy took risks, so did the Reverend William A. Holmes, whose words you heard read a few minutes ago. In the same sermon he reported that some fourth-grade children in Dallas had clapped and cheered when their teacher told them the President had been shot and killed. As a result of Holmes's speaking out, he and his family had to leave their home for a while and have police protection.

What do you feel was the significance of the action of these children? How can we try to prevent such "echoes" in the future? Or will we rationalize and "wash our hands of it"?

Prayer:

Dear Lord, we turn to thee, knowing that we cannot condemn the people of Dallas, for many a time we have "washed our hands" of a situation that looked dangerous or would take effort. Help us to have concern for the big issues that confront our nation and waste less time on petty ones that seem more important. Help us to speak words based on fact rather than feeling, words that will not run the risk of instilling wrong ideas in the minds of children too young to grasp their significance.

It is not we who seek to do this on our own. We know this is thy way, O Lord; so make us instruments of thy will and give us additional strength and tenacity to take a stand whenever the situation arises.

Cast out our little hates and prejudices and fill us with the loving concern for all men, taught to us by thy Son, Jesus Christ, in whose name we pray. Amen.

3. TEN COMMANDMENTS ON HOW BEST TO UNDERMINE AMERICA

Scripture: Jude 1:5, 10-13 ("Fruitless trees in late autumn.")

Reading:

"(1) Above all, *hate*—anything and everybody, especially the underdog. (2) Cause as much chaos and dissention as possible. Show the world that a democracy or a republic can bring forth no accord. (3) Continue to call yourself a Christian or a Jew, but do not in *any* way act to abide by the dictates of the Judeo-Christian principles. (4) Despise the United Nations. Continue to manufacture slogans such as 'Get the U.S. Out of the U.N.' (5) Believe in no such absurdities as morality, virtue, honor, justice, love. Cheat whenever you can. (6) Call anyone who disagrees with you 'communist' or 'nigger lover' or whatever term you can hope to bow the person down with. (7) Separate all who are not like you *from* you; in division there is weakness. (8) Talk down foreign aid: its gifts and/or loans often create friends for the donor. (9) Seek after personal pleasure for the moment. Do not look ahead. [Confine] education to acquiring skills by which you can earn a wealth of *things*. (10) Remain silent, apathetic. Don't think at all. Thinking might produce concern. Concern might prove disastrous." [3]

Suggestions for Discussion and Action:

The Letter of Jude is short. It was written at a time when the moral standards of Christians were being threatened, as the new religion spread to people of quite different backgrounds and ideals. There is always a danger of the lowering of standards as numbers get larger. The same thing has happened in our country, where the strictness of the Puritans has been undermined by the steady infiltration of thousands of people of different backgrounds and ideals.

The imagery in verses twelve and thirteen could well apply to the constant movement of people in America today.

It is much easier to write a negative list, such as these "Ten Commandments," than a positive one. Try compiling a list of your own as an antidote, not a theoretical one, but ten active suggestions for combating the weaknesses so graphically portrayed.

Then, try carrying some of them out!

Prayer:

Lord God, arouse us from our apathy, help us to think with concern and compassion, root us firmly with reasons for our actions, and let the world see that we live under the rule of God with justice and love for our fellow men, irrespective of color or creed. Amen.

4. THE ROOT OF BITTERNESS

Scripture: Deut. 29:16-18 ("A root bearing poisonous and bitter fruit.")

Reading:

What do we do when we meet people full of bitter hate? Try to keep out of their way, usually. How do we feel when we read about "hate" groups or see pictures of them in the press or on TV? Reject them, usually, as "odd-balls," as part of a minority who make the news because they are sick, sick.

Sometimes we apply amateur psychology, and decide it is good for the person full of hatred to get it out of his system. So we listen, and say nothing. Such a negative, or passive, reaction can lead that person to feel his listener agrees with him and even to tell others that he does! On the other hand, he can also feel he is not being taken seriously, and his bitterness increases.

We Americans pride ourselves on our tolerance, on the constitutional right of freedom of expression for every citizen. Sometimes, we forget to use our *own* freedom to express what we feel, and so our tolerance can be a form of laziness.

Blind, irrational hate is becoming a real problem in our country, and we can no longer ignore it. The reaction to a story published by the *Ladies' Home Journal*, has helped the general public become more aware of it.

"The Children's Story" was written by James Clavell, and published in October, 1963. It told, in fictional form, what could happen in America if it were conquered by an unknown enemy. A school class waits apprehensively, with its teacher, for her replacement by someone from the New Enemy. Expecting a cold figure in jack-boots cracking a whip, they are relieved when an attractive young woman appears.

The new teacher is gentle and kind, but thoroughly prepared. She already knows the name of each child, which relaxes them even more; but she confuses them over the oath of the allegiance to the flag. She suggests they cut the flag in pieces, so that each one can take a bit home as a souvenir. The values of the children are carefully changed from the spiritual to the material. She tells them to pray to God for candy, and when none appears, suggests they pray to "our Leader" for some. While their eyes are closed, she produces some herself. One child sees through this trick, but she praises him for his perception, and wins him to her side too.

The editors published the story because they felt it was a fine example of the dangers of subversion in a velvet glove instead of a clenched fist, and that this might be a way of warning people that a friendly enemy can be deceptive.

To their amazement, the editors received a flood of abusive mail, accusing them of propaganda against God and country! They wrote: "What distressed us in this flood of mail was not its disagreement with a story we had run. A living magazine must occasionally risk such disagreement from its readers. But a living magazine cannot stand idly by and neglect to comment on as many as 2,000 letters written as thoughtless and primitive responses to an inaccurate directive from a single person." [4]

This "single person" was Robert Welch, founder of the John Birch Society, who warned his followers that "The Children's Story" would "lull Americans to sleep about Communism." [5]

The shocking thing was that many of those who wrote the most vituperative letters boasted that they refused to read such a story! Editors were told to return to Russia, that the F.B.I. had been informed, as well as incoherent abuse for the United States Supreme Court, President Kennedy, the United Nations, the nuclear-test ban, and fluoridation.

The *Journal* followed its policy of answering every letter that gave a return address. As well as this, they printed Mr. Clavell's own explanation. This merely threw fat on the fire. Fifty-eight replied, with even more hysteria, refusing to accept any explanation.

The *Journal* considered the whole matter serious enough for a special article, "A Report to Our Readers," which appeared in the April 1964 issue.

Suggestions for Discussion and Action:

What does this story say to us as Christians?

Read Prov. 8:1-9 ("O foolish man, pay attention.")

After you have discussed ideas from your group, add any of these that were not included:

Hate usually comes from fear. *Fear* usually comes from ignorance. *Ignorance* usually comes from lack of relevant education. *Politics* is a branch of education Christians usually neglect! Isn't it about time they became better informed? Isn't it about time Christians learned how to talk back?

Plan some action, either related to better information on political issues—local, national, international, or some specific "hate" situation or group in your community.

Close with this prayer, based on Heb. 12:12-15.

Prayer:

May the God of peace lift our drooping hands and strengthen our weak knees and make straight paths for our feet, so that what is lame may not be put out of joint but rather be healed. May we strive for peace with all men, and for the holiness without which no one will see God; that no "root of bitterness" spring up and cause trouble, enabling any to become defiled. We pray through Jesus Christ, to whom be glory for ever and ever. Amen.

5. WAS ANNE FRANK'S FATHER APATHETIC?

Scripture: Eph. 6:10-13 ("Having done all, to stand.")

Reading:

There must be few people who have not read *The Diary of Anne Frank,* seen the play, or seen the movie based on it. It is a moving story—that has aroused the feelings of many—of a teen-age girl who tried hard to adjust herself and her life to living in an attic, hiding from the Nazis. Her only view of the outside world was a patch of sky that changed with the seasons and the weather. Anne's father planned this hideout with great care in an effort to keep his family and their way of life intact. It has touched many parents with the feeling that this is what they would have done too, in similar circumstances.

This feeling was rudely shattered when Bruno Bettelheim wrote an article, in the November, 1960, issue of *Harper's,* called "The Ignored Lesson of Anne Frank." Here Dr. Bettelheim, who had been imprisoned at Dachau and Buchenwald himself, stated that Mr. Frank's action was blind and apathetic. He had clung to the conviction that, if they could all stay together and keep their pattern of family life unchanged, "everything would be alright." He feels they were typical of many Jewish families who should have made plans for flight and survival, even though it meant splitting up the family unit in order to do so. Why *didn't* the Franks try to escape from Holland when there was still time?

Dr. Bettelheim continued with his belief that many Jews allowed themselves to be taken away to concentration camps, and allowed themselves to be led into gas chambers, with ever-increasing apathy as conditions grew more hopeless. At the same time, they clung to little everyday happenings and blotted out any wider views to such a degree that it weakened their sense of values. For example, he said that some prisoners ate their food ration the moment they got it and collapsed at the end of the day. They could not take evil seriously and held on to "wishful thinking." They could no longer look ahead and see the inevitability of their death.

Dr. Bettelheim does not blame Anne Frank for what he calls her "senseless fate." She faced her situation with courage, but it was wasted courage. She died "because her parents could not get themselves to believe in Auschwitz. And her story found wide acclaim because for us too, it denies implicitly that Auschwitz ever existed. If all men are good, there never was an Auschwitz." [6]

We need to think about this accusation of a similar lack in us, and a desire to pretend there is no evil, no hate directed against us that will not go away if we live right.

The article caused a great furor, for it made it seem as if all Jews were cowards. One writer expostulated that Dr. Bettelheim forgot to mention the conviction of the devout Jew, that there is no greater honor than submissive martyrdom to sanctify the Name. A Jew must be worthy, if he is called, to undergo any kind of suffering. He believes it actually furthers the purpose of God, as well as giving profound meaning to the life of the sufferer.

Whether we agree that the Franks were foolish, or not, Dr. Bettelheim's theory should make us stop and think. Are there times when it is right to hate? Times when we need to do more than hope for the best, or accept our fate meekly? Dietrich Bonhoeffer, who was himself killed by the Nazis, thought about this very deeply, and decided there are times when a Christian must "sin boldly," and so he joined a plot to overthrow the Nazi hierarchy.

To us, who follow the New Testament, the passage in Ephesians has a special message. Can we say, that "having done all," we stand? Or do we just stand?

Suggestions for Discussion and Action:

Are we all inclined to be like Anne Frank's father at times? Is there something similar here, in the building of family fall-out shelters as much "like home" as possible?

Look at the Jewish belief on purposeful suffering. How does it differ from our Christian beliefs? God does not ask man to sacrifice his life for him. Jesus Christ made the supreme sacrifice of his life for all men, once and for all; although a man may readily sacrifice his life in defense of his Christian beliefs.

What should we react against, more strongly than we do, for the betterment of mankind—including the welfare of those closest to us? War, communism, highway deaths, radioactive fallout, protection against sexual perverts, lung cancer—there are many others. No one is apathetic enough to walk in front of a speeding car, but does the law in your community take sufficient action against speeding drivers?

Is apathy a real sickness, whose symptom is easy rationalism? "I would do something if I could." "I don't feel it is my affair."

"I'll start tomorrow." In the Gospel of John, Jesus finds a man lying by a pool where the paralyzed went in to bathe, and he asks if he wants to be healed. "The sick man answered him, 'Sir, I have no man to put me into the pool when the water is troubled, and while I am going another steps down before me.' Jesus said to him, 'Rise, take up your pallet, and walk.' And at once the man was healed, and he took up his pallet and walked" (John 5:7-9).

Did Jesus heal this man's paralysis, or his apathy about it?

Think of some course of action out in your community, about which you, or everyone, has been apathetic.

Prayer:

O Lord God, forgive us that so often we try to forget about the inhumanity of man, the suffering of the innocent, and the outcome of hate. Forgive us that we prefer to read about pleasant things, and too often assume that there is exaggeration where there is not. Help us to keep alert and well informed, so that we are ready to do all we can to prevent such things in your world. Give us the courage to know when to "sin boldly" in defense of the oppressed, and arm us against the tyranny of evil. In the name of Christ, we pray. Amen.

6. WE DO NOT MAKE ROOM

Scripture: Luke 2:4-7, NEB

"Joseph went up to Judaea from the town of Nazareth in Galilee, to be registered at the city of David, called Bethlehem, because he was of the house of David by descent; and with him went Mary who was bethrothed to him. She was pregnant, and while they were there the time came for her child to be born, and she gave birth to a son, her first-born. She wrapped him round, and laid him in a manger, because there was no room for them to lodge in the house."

Reading:

There was praise from many for the teen-age members of the Demolay chapter in Los Alamos, when they refused to promise their adult advisers that they would blackball a Negro applicant for membership. Their charter was later withdrawn. Because the boy was a Negro, the news made headlines, but how many times have other white boys been blackballed upon the advice of advisers, or by members themselves, who did not consider them "suitable"? What are the feelings of young people, irrespective of color, when they are rejected as not being "good enough" for a fraternity or sorority? What does it feel like to be "left out" of a club, or even the crowd at the malt shop? What does it feel like to know others are accepted, but there is no room for you? Did Lee Harvey Oswald feel this way?

When Hitler began to persecute the Jews in Germany in 1939, there was a frantic exodus by rail, sea, air, and foot, but relatively few were admitted to the Western countries.

Nine hundred men, women, and children set sail, on the S.S. "St. Louis," for Cuba, but their visas were canceled, and the Cuban government turned them away. The "St. Louis" sailed from country to country, from port to port, and its passengers became desperate. No country would allow them to leave their ship. At last, France, Great Britain, and the Netherlands agreed to each take a third, although they were facing food rationing; but many Jews were sent back to Germany and killed. Why would America not make room for them?

It was a warm spring night in the big city. The screams of a woman were heard over the continual babel of many TV sets. A few heads looked out of windows, a few gathered on the street and stood there looking mildly curious. The woman called for help, her voice grew weaker and finally stopped. The people closed their windows or went back indoors. The show was over. They returned to the show on TV.

Next day, the news reported that the woman was stabbed to

death. Why did no one care enough to go and help her, or call the police? Why did no one make room for her on the safe side of the street?

During World War II Maude Royden once said, "I used to be a pacifist. I know now that I would rather go to hell for fighting than have my son grow up to think it was funny to kick a Jew in the stomach." [7]

Jesus said, "Behold, I stand at the door and knock" (Rev. 3:20).

If we do not make room for our fellow men, how can we make room for Jesus Christ? If we make room for Jesus Christ, we know we *must* make room for our fellow men.

Suggestions for Discussion and Action:

You may want to add a few similar items from the current news. After discussion, what action might you want to take? How about an antidiscriminatory code of your own? (Remember that color discrimination is only one of the problems.)

Check with the Anti-defamation League. Have a few of your members prepared to give a report on conditions in South Africa, among German youth, or any other current problem areas abroad.

Prayer: (based on Rom. 7:15-19)

Almighty God, we come before you in bewilderment at the things we think and say and do, which we do not intend to think or say or do. Strengthen us, so that we understand our own actions more fully, as individuals and as members of this group. Help us to know what good we should try to do and do it, through thy son Jesus Christ. Amen.

7. THE DISGRACE OF SILENCE

Scripture: Mark 14:26-30, 66-72 ("I neither know nor understand what you mean.")

Reading:

If we were asked which man was guilty of the most evil in the New Testament, we would immediately think of Judas, the man who has become the symbol of betrayal. But what about the denial of Peter? No one could call him evil, yet he was guilty of one of the more insidious sins—that of refusing to become involved, of pretending to know nothing, or just saying and doing nothing. Perhaps we are inclined to belittle Peter's lack of courage, because we have all been guilty of the disgrace of silence too.

Peter denied association with Christ, and we do this too, in a more subtle way, as we refuse to do what we know we should do as Christians. It's so easy, inside the church building! Outside is quite different. Here again we are like Peter, for he was so sure of his convictions while surrounded by the other disciples, but lost his courage when he was alone in a hostile environment.

When are we like Peter? Do you remember the time four little girls were killed by a bomb in a Birmingham church? Everyone was shocked. Everyone said it was, of course, the work of extremists. Everyone blamed the incident on a few people, and did not link it with the result of political or economical blight, for which they were responsible. However, a few people spoke up. One, a young lawyer, said this, to the Birmingham Young Man's Business Club:

"Four little girls were killed in Birmingham yesterday. An aroused, remorseful, worried community asks, 'Who did it? Who threw that bomb? Was it a Negro or a white?'

"The answer should be, 'We all did it.' Every last one of us is condemned for that crime and for the bombing before it and for the one last month, last year, a decade ago. We all did it. . . .

"But, you know, the answer to 'Who did it?' is really rather simple. The 'who' is every individual who talks about the 'niggers' and spreads the seeds of his hate to his neighbor, to his son. The 'who' is the jokester, the crude oaf whose racial jokes rock the party with laughter. The 'who' is every governor who ever shouted for lawlessness and became a violator of the law. The 'who' is every senator and every representative who, in the halls of Congress, stands and with mock humility tells the world that things back home aren't really as they are. The 'who' is the courts that move ever so slowly, the newspapers that timorously defend the law. The 'who' is all the Christians and all their ministers who spoke too late in anguished cries against the violence. The 'who' is the coward in each of us who clucks admonitions. . . .

"Who is really guilty? Each of us. . . . Every person in this community who has, in any way, contributed during the past several years to the popularity of hatred is at least as guilty, or more so, than the demented fool who threw that bomb." [8]

This disgraceful silence is not confined to our generation. It happened in Germany in World War II in much more dreadful circumstances. Rabbi Joachim Prinz was with the Jewish community in Berlin, under the Hitler regime. He spoke at the Freedom March in Washington, D.C. in 1963, and said:

"The most important thing that I learned in my life and under those tragic circumstances is that bigotry and hatred are not the most urgent problem.

"The most urgent, the most disgraceful, the most shameful and the most tragic problem is silence. A great people which had become a great civilization had become a nation of silent onlookers. They remained silent in the face of hate, in the face of brutality and in the face of murder." [9]

Perhaps the crimes committed in Nazi Germany seem far away. After all, it is over twenty years since D-day, and the grass has grown again. We have other things to think about—but did the adults of that time think deeply about the atrocities? Their words were a sham of shock over inner complacency. A play called *The Deputy*, written recently by a young German, has stirred up this complacency and exposed the guilt feelings. *The Deputy* has aroused antagonism and caused controversy wherever it has been produced—in Berlin, London or New York—because the playwright, Rolf Hochhuth, contends that Pope Pius XII was guilty of silence when he should have spoken about the massacre of over six million Jews.

Albert Schweitzer pointed out that the failure to speak, and to accept inhumanity, belongs to the Protestant as well as the Roman Catholic Church. In spite of themselves, men began to see that we are *all* guilty.

Suggestions for Discussion and Action:

You may think it ridiculous to blame ourselves for incidents that took place on the other side of the world over twenty years ago. You may wonder what we can do now, anyhow.

Action has been taken, in a very practical way by the International Christian Settlement in Israel, called "Nes Ammim." Here, a number of Christians have decided to work side by side with the new beginnings of the Jewish people, to express their remorse for the persecutions and for antisemitism. A village-community has been established, composed of international and interdenominational worker. The organization originated in Switzerland and Israel, but there now is a US-Nes Ammim Committee. This is Christian action in a very real way, and it is interesting to note that at first the Israel government was a little hesitant, for it was afraid this might be a missionary venture. Now that it is sure the intent is to work with them, the government is giving assistance with roads, water, etc.

Whether anyone in your group might be interested in working in a project of this kind, or not, discuss it in relation to the link we know exists between our actions as individuals and the actions of groups of people, governments, and nations.

Read the scripture again. Although the circumstances were different (for Peter was denying his Lord), the end result was the same. *Peter had not the courage to get involved.*

What action can you take that will involve your time, your energy, your outspoken convictions—even in the face of criticism and rebuke? What can you do for the helpless, the hopeless, the down-trodden, and those who deliberately turn from the church as a place of refuge and help?

Prayer:

O Lord God, confront us with the guilt of complacent silence; with the hypocrisy of always laying the blame before others; with our unwillingness to acknowledge our responsibility for many things that we dismiss as distasteful and of no concern to us. Give us the gift of insistence for the truth, compassionate love, and a zeal to stamp out evil. In the name of Christ we ask it. Amen.

8. CASTING BLACK AND WHITE STONES

Scripture: John 7:53–8:11 ("Let him who is without sin among you be the first to throw a stone.")

Reading:

Some years ago Norman Cousins, editor of the *Saturday Review*, spoke to a group of students in Pakistan.[10] He followed his speech with the usual time for questions. Suddenly a student rose to his feet with a violent attack on what he called the dishonest and untruthful stories Mr. Cousins had been telling them about the United States.

The head of the college apologized profusely for such a display of bad manners, but Mr. Cousins asked that the student be allowed to continue, as he wanted everyone to speak freely.

The student had not expected this and seemed reluctant to get to his feet again. Finally he did, and cried out that if the speaker had been really honest in his talk he would have admitted all the ugly things his people did to those Americans who did not happen to have a white skin. At that moment the audience changed, as if a spark of electricity had run through it.

This situation was not new to Norman Cousins. He had been warned about it before he left the States, and soon found that no matter what subject he spoke on, the issue of race prejudice in the United States always came up.

So he sat and listened while the student poured out all the tales he had heard about segregated schools, inferior housing, and the lack of jobs.

The student declared that each insult to someone of another color in the United States was an insult to everyone of another color in the rest of the world. One day Americans would discover that the peoples of India and China and Japan and South America were not inferior. One day Americans would discover they were alone, and that the majority of the world's people would no longer put up with fancy talk of superiority.

When Mr. Cousins made his reply, he began by agreeing that, certainly, race prejudice existed in the United States and was a serious problem. He said it was important, however, to make a distinction between what was actually happening, and the distorted, exaggerated accounts prepared by Red propaganda and even by some of the press in Pakistan.

He went on to tell the students that Americans were very definitely doing something to eradicate the evil of segregation. Progress was admittedly not fast enough, but the important thing to remember was that work was being done.

Mr. Cousins pointed out that the problem of prejudice was not a uniquely American one. It was the problem of that bitter, corroding feeling that existed inside all people when they felt they had certain privileges and wanted to deny them to others. It existed when he saw signs in hotels in Bombay saying, "South Africans not admitted." It existed where national laws were passed about untouchability. In Pakistan itself, he had found evidence of both religious intolerance and prejudice. Where minorities were concerned, there was a distinct prejudice against the Sikhs.

The response to his speech was remarkable. The students had not seen the situation in this light before. Afterwards Mr. Cousins had a friendly discussion with the antagonistic student, who said he felt his questions had been answered, but considered the United States was at fault in not letting the rest of the world know what it was doing.

This happened in 1951. We have come a long way since then, but how far have we come in admitting that we are all prone to have feelings of prejudice?

Suggestions for Discussion and Action:

This account of Norman Cousins in Pakistan should interest us in two ways. Firstly, he let the student speak freely, and then assumed it gave him the right to speak freely also, so there was genuine communication between them. Secondly, he made it clear that we dare not judge others blindly, for there is no area where we cannot be judged too.

How does this relate to foreign students visiting our country? Have you had any genuine communication with some of them? Or have you merely listened to them talk about their country? (Preferably, in national dress and separated from you by a podium or platform. Try doing that yourself sometime, and you will find it preventing any chance of empathy or communication!)

Can you plan some way in which you can offer more than hospitality to foreign students? Try to become alert to their unvoiced needs or inner confusions in a strange country. For example: A Filipino student at an American university had her billfold stolen. It contained all the money for her tuition, and she was about to go back home. A group of her classmates did ironing, sold flowers, and organized other money-making projects to replace the amount, and she was able to stay.

How many in your group have been "foreign students"? See Chapter IX for opportunities to be one during the summer vacation or longer.

Prayer: (with apologies to Robert Burns)

O Lord, give us the grace to see ourselves as others see us, and the sense to learn from it. Amen.

ADDITIONAL WORSHIP RESOURCES

Scripture:

Rom. 2:1 ("You have no excuse . . . when you judge another.")

Col. 3:1-15 ("Love, which binds everything together.")

Eph. 2:12-22 ("He . . . has broken down the dividing wall of hostility.")

Eph. 4:25-32 ("Let all bitterness and wrath and anger . . . be put away.")

Gal. 2:11-21 ("Cephas . . . drew back.")

Gal. 3:25-28 ("All are one in Christ Jesus.")

Gal. 5:19-24 ("The works of the flesh are: . . . strife, jealousy, anger, selfishness.")

Jer. 50:6-7 ("We are not guilty, for they have sinned.")

Ps. 14 ("There is none that does good, no, not one.")

Ps. 15 ("He who . . . does no evil to his friend.")

Isa. 59:1-9 ("Their works are works of iniquity.")

Prov. 19 ("Good sense makes a man slow to anger.")

Prayer:

"A Litany for Justice and Good Human Relations."

"*Leader:* Almighty God, who hast created all men in thy own image; and receivest with joy the worship of all nations, classes, and races of men:

"*People:* We praise thee, our God and Creator.

"*Leader:* O thou who dost rule and judge with equity and justice the contending wills of thy rebellious creatures:

"*People:* We praise thee, our God and our Judge.

"*Leader:* O thou whose grace and mercy save without distinction all who come to thee in Jesus Christ:

"*People:* We praise thee, our God and Redeemer.

"*Leader:* We come to thee acknowledging our oneness in creation, in sin, and in hope, with those whom men call different from us:

"*People:* Hear us, we beseech thee, O Lord.

"*Leader:* We come to thee rejoicing in our uniqueness as persons in one human family—living and loving, seeking and striving, fearing and hoping—each in his own way:

"*People:* Hear us, we beseech thee, O Lord.

"*Leader:* For our demanding of others what we are unwilling to do ourselves, for our easy professions of love unmatched by difficult acts of justice, for our pretensions of understanding in the midst of our ignorance:

"*People:* Forgive us and help us, O Lord.

"*Leader:* For our disclaimers of prejudice in ourselves and our enjoyment of the fruits of prejudice in others, for our refusal to lead the way until others first reform, for our pious benevolence that leaves the structures of injustice unchanged:

"*People:* Forgive us and help us, O Lord.

"*Leader:* For the sense of superiority disguised by acts of charity, for the preference for peace instead of struggle for equity, for the abundance of words when talk is easy and the abundance of silence when witness is costly:

"*People:* Forgive us and help us, O Lord. . . .

"*Leader:* For the shaking of our own complacency; for thy love that will not let us go; for our hope in Jesus Christ:

"*People:* We praise thee and thank thee, our Heavenly Father.

"*Leader and People:* Eternal God and Father of us all, hasten the day when we and all men, differing in color, creed, and clan, shall recognize our common origin, need, and destiny in thee, and dwell together in brotherhood with justice in the earth. Bless thou every effort, and forgive the failures, to move toward this goal; and, beginning with us, who need and claim thy mercy in Jesus Christ, replace words with deeds and sentiments with sacrifice, for we pray in the name of the same Jesus Christ our Lord. Amen." [11]

Hymns:

Once to Every Man and Nation
Faith of Our Fathers
Believe Not Those Who Say the Upward Path Is Smooth
Be Strong!
Christ of the Upward Way
He Who Would Valiant Be
Herald's of Christ Who Bear the King's Commands
God of Grace and God of Glory
A Mighty Fortress Is Our God

chapter V

THE CHANGING PATTERNS OF WORK

1. BE WORTHY OF YOUR HIRE

Scripture: Rom. 14:5-8 ("None of us lives to himself.")

Reading:

Rules for work in 1872, from the proprietor of a carriage and wagon works in the state of Washington.

1: Office employees will daily sweep the floors, dust the furniture, shelves and showcases.

2: Each day fill lamps, clean chimneys and trim wicks. Wash the windows once a week.

3. Each clerk will bring in a bucket of water and a scuttle of coal for the day's business.

4: Make your pens carefully. You may whittle nibs to your individual taste.

5: This office will open at 7 a.m. and close at 8 p.m. daily, except on the Sabbath, on which day it will remain closed. Each employee is expected to spend the Sabbath by attending church and contributing liberally to the cause of the Lord.

6: Men employees will be given an evening off each week for courting purposes, or two evenings a week if they go regularly to church.

7: After an employee has spent 13 hours of labor in the office, he should spend the time reading the Bible and other good books while contemplating the Glories and building up of the Kingdom.

8: Every employee should lay aside from each pay a goodly sum of his earnings for his benefit during his declining years, so that he will not become a burden upon the charity of his betters.

9: Any employee who smokes Spanish cigars, uses liquor in any form, gets shaved at a barber shop, or frequents pool and public halls, will give me a good reason to suspect his worth, intentions, integrity and honesty.

10: The employee who has performed his labors faithfully and without fault for a period of five years in my service, and who has been thrifty and attentive to his religious duties, is looked upon by his fellowmen as a substantial and law-abiding citizen, will be given an increase of five cents per day in his pay, providing a just return in profits from the business permits it.

11: Be worthy of your hire.

(Signed ZACHARY U. GEIGER, Sole Proprietor, Mt. Cory Carriage and Wagon Works, April 5, 1872)[1]

Suggestions for Discussion and Action:

This reading will probably be received with amazement and amusement! Here you find a Christian employer having a real grip on the life of those who work for him. How does this differ from recent efforts to relate the church to life in the workaday world? How did these people compare with those in our comfortable churches today?

After some general discussion try to guide the group toward exploration of that word "Sabbath." You might want to assign three people to look up the definition of these three words before your meeting takes place—"Sunday," in an encyclopedia; "sabbath," Exod. 20:8-11; Matt. 12:1-13; Mark 2:23-28; and "the Lord's Day," Acts 16:11-15; 20:7-12; I Cor. 16:1-2; Rev. 1:10.

How do you feel Sunday should be observed? What about Sunday closing hours and laws? How much is your church building used on that day and by whom? Does your group meet on that evening? If so, why?

You may find it easy to criticize the sabbath practices of a century ago. Try to find some good that we have lost today. Try to come to a deeper understanding of this day, and perhaps, some totally different way of observing it, as families, or as your group, which you feel will have more significance to your lives as Christians.

Prayer:

O Lord God, help us to penetrate the purpose of our habits and discover if they need to be changed, not for the sake of change, but in order to give them life and meaning, and glory to thy name. Amen.

2. THE MEANING OF WORK

Scripture: Isa. 28:24-26

"Does he who plows for sowing plow continually?
does he continually open and harrow his ground?
When he has leveled its surfaces,
does he not scatter dill, sow cummin,

and put wheat in rows
and barley in its proper place,
and spelt as the border?
For he is instructed aright;
his God teaches him."

Reading:

Paul S. Minear has called the Bible "a book by workers, about workers, for workers." [2] We know this, but we like to think it refers to workers who lived in the days when the Bible was written, having little connection with our materialistic world today. After all, there is not much relationship between those who "put . . . barley in its proper place" and one of the seventeen thousand job classifications needed to produce a single can of peas! (Or is there?) Perhaps Paul Minear is also right when he says that "the Bible may contain messages which God addresses to us at our daily business, but seldom do we hear His voice above the whir of modern machines." [3]

What kind of messages does God address to us at work? A reminder to go to church next Sunday or to pray for the alleviation of a personal problem?

When we think of "God" and "work" together, do these words come instantly to mind—"job," "hard sell," "boss," "overtime," "unions," "white collar," or "paycheck"? Are we not more apt to think of "calling" or "vocation," seeing a minister in a pulpit or a missionary preparing to go to some far-flung country?

"Early Christians did not so much speak of a person going to church, but more often thought of the church as being present with each person at his place of daily employment. . . . In his chores were embodied its repentance and forgiveness, its struggle with temptation, its victory. . . . Thus early Christians located the frontier of God's war along the line of human associations and decisions encountered in their day-to-day living. They were called to give their witness to the emancipating power of the gospel in the freedom and joy within which they accomplished their routine jobs. Faith produced a quiet revolution in all their attitudes toward the ordinary work situation." [4]

Today, God does not call a man to be a plumber or a biologist, a garment worker or a housewife. He calls a man to follow him no matter what his line of work may be. He called Paul to be an apostle—not a tentmaker. It's as simple as that.

The answer to this call cannot be restricted to Sundays and other special times. It must percolate through every part of life, or the call is not heeded.

Suggestions for Discussion and Action:

Read the scripture again. Notice the awareness of the different skills and techniques, as being taught by God.

How can we link together the world of the Bible, in a different time and place, with the world of contemporary America? You have probably grown up learning many stories from the Bible that seem to have the same degree of unreality as a fairy tale— Joseph and his coat of many colors, or Moses in the bullrushes. When you were a child, what did the twenty-third psalm create in your mind? Had you ever seen a shepherd? If the first line had been changed to, "The Lord is my school bus driver," would you have had greater understanding?

We need to do this with reference to work today. Any work any of you may do (and not necessarily the lifework you will choose)—baby-sitting, toting groceries, writing a theme, operating an elevator—"Whatever you do, do all to the glory of God" (I Cor. 10:31).

Read the selected passage from Isaiah again and change the words to some stages of work or techniques you perform, as a group or as individuals.

Prayer:

"Teach me, my God and King,
In all things Thee to see,
And what I do in any thing
To do it as for Thee.

A servant with this clause
Makes drudgery divine;
Who sweeps a room, as for Thy laws,
Makes that and the action fine." [5]

3. SEPTEMBER

Scripture: Rom. 12:3-13 ("Having gifts that differ.")

Reading: (by a group of different voices)
"This is the time of the year
When the earth is shifting gear,
A time when the leaves are dry,
And grasshoppers rub their knees.

"An end to things, yet a start;
When swallows gather and wait,
With chatter, on telephone wires;
Line up, and dive, and come back,
Increasing in numbers each day,
Preparing to make their flight
To the uttermost ends of the earth.
Yet the flight of the swallow is blind,
With a drive from instinct alone.
No reason, no map and no plan,
They simply know they must go,
And many have gone before.

"Under the telephone wires
The young people gather too.
They also chatter and wait,
With expectancy in the air,
New clothes, new books and new shoes,
New teachers, new subjects ahead.

And maybe they groan about school
(For that they're expected to do),
But under it all is an urge,
As they move on, to learn something new.
To find, to discover, to seek
For the way they are meant to go,
In their search for a job for life.
Some have decided by now;
The air force, a doctor, a nurse,
A teacher, a preacher, a coach.
And some are still looking for clues.
'I know that I'm no good at math,
But I think I could work with my hands . . .'
'I like to meet people and talk . . .'
'I can't seem to spell, though I try . . .'
'Fix a car's about all *I* can do . . .'
'I like the outdoors, could I farm?'
'I mean to learn more about space,
Astro-physics might help me along . . .'
'I admit that my aim is to marry,
But cooking and cleaning, I *hate*!'
'I don't know yet *what* I will do . . .
so maybe I'd better enlist!'

"Quite unlike all the swallows above,
They each seek a purpose and plan,
A desire to know what to do,
Whether wealthy, or gifted, or slow.
Each one has his worth and his place,
And each has his chance to attempt
The daring or difficult thing.
And each has the chance to become
The best he is able to be.
Each has his chance to give God
Of his best, in return for his life." [6]

117

Suggestions for Discussion and Action:

Read the scripture again.

How can you, "with sober judgment," assess the gifts God has given you, and decide how best to use them?

Jobs are scarce—you already know that.

Higher education or manual training is a must—you already know that.

If you are an American male, physically and mentally fit, Uncle Sam may need you for a while—you already know that.

Everyone accepts those first two statements. Why do they sigh at the thought of the third? The verses you have just heard had a line which read, "So maybe I'd better enlist!" Not exactly burning with patriotism, is it? Is it because everyone wants to get this education business over with and start earning a living? Or is it because Americans hate being forced to do something?

Discuss this from the viewpoint of the preamble to the Constitution of the United States: "Insure domestic tranquility, provide for the common defence, promote the general Welfare, and secure the Blessings of Liberty to ourselves and our posterity." Have we lost sight of the meaning of the word "service"?

Unless we admit to being the comfortable kind of Christian, don't we all feel the need for some opportunity to be of service? Being trained to defend your country should be a privilege, and so is being trained to serve in the Peace Corps or in any project that will help the helpless.

During the last few years, six thousand German young people have given a year of service. Some came straight from school, and some from the universities, but many actually gave up their jobs. Why did they do this? The Evangelical Church in Germany reports that some wanted time for reflection or fellowship, some wanted to help other people and learn something new. Some said they were looking for a way of life which could be a vocation instead of just a job in which they earned money. And only half of them returned to what they were doing before. The rest decided to make a career in some form of service.

Chapter IX contains information about service opportunities all over the world, close to home, for several years, or a few weeks. One pamphlet you could obtain has the good title of *"Invest Your Summer."*

Prayer:

"We pray now, O Father, to be used roughly. Stamp on our selfishness. Chill our warm and comfortable content with things as they are. Frighten us with an awareness of our new power to destroy ourselves and frustrate God's purpose for his children. Open our eyes to the opportunities for great and marvelous achievement which lie at our hands. And fill us with urgency and zeal to accomplish what we have in us to do in the years which have been provided us. In Jesus' name. Amen." [7]

4. ON BEING A "PROPER CHRISTIAN"

Scripture: Phil. 4:8-13 ("Think about these things.")

Reading:

A recent book, *God's Frozen People*, refers to the lay people of today whose faith seems to be taken out of the refrigerator on a Sunday morning and then put back again. They do not take it with them to the factory at 7:15 or to the board meeting at 9:30.

The authors of this book feel this may just be a failure of moral courage: "A great number of men feel that they cannot honestly be a 'proper Christian' at work and keep their jobs. They must keep their jobs—if only for the sake of their wives and families. So they assume that they just can't be 'proper' Christians; and since hypocrisy is, thank God, one of the most disliked attitudes among men today, they feel it much better not to pretend to be particularly Christian about their daily work. They would rather just be

119

considered 'decent types,' and leave it at that. To be a 'Christian,' a 'religious type,' would mean either becoming a hopelessly pious Bible-puncher, or pretending to some kind of 100 percent perfectionism *which they know they can't achieve* as salesmen, as bus drivers, or even as school teachers." [8]

All this comes from the strange idea many people still have, outside the church as well as in it, that unless you are "good" you are not a "good Christian!"

How can a man be a Christian in his work?

"He must serve his neighbor on the job—his fellow workers. . . .

"He must serve his customer—directly . . . and indirectly if he designs, or grows, or assembles, or paints, or packs articles which eventually a customer will buy. . . . He must serve the firm or public authority he works for. . . . He must serve the community in which he works and lives. . . . He must serve his 'calling'—he must respect and try to add to the knowledge and learning and skill and traditional know-how in his particular job.[9]

Suggestions for Discussion and Action:

Read the scripture again in another translation, by J. B. Phillips or in the New English Bible. Concentrate on the line, "think on these things" (or "fix your mind," or "fill all your thoughts with these things)."

There is a picture called "The Soul's Awakening" which used to be very popular fifty years ago. It showed a young girl clasping a Bible, with her eyes raised to heaven in a state of bliss. It was not a good picture to have around the house, for the eyes of the girl were transfixed. She seemed unable to get past that state of bliss and start living. (Perhaps she was also one of "God's Frozen People.") However, we should not make snide remarks about her, for we can easily become transfixed in the same state ourselves, except that we call it not "bliss," but a "mountaintop experience." We can stay up there, thinking pure and lovely thoughts, but is this enough?

How can we transpose our pure and lovely thoughts into everyday work situations that are far from being pure and lovely?

Is it true that we feel we are not good enough unless we are 100 percent perfect? Do we get this feeling because of the mistaken idea, held by many non-Christians, that Christians consider themselves a cut above everyone else? Is it not, rather, the other way round? Are not Christians the community of those who admit their inadequacy and sinfulness? We might remember that even Jesus objected to being called "good," when he said, "Why do you call me good? No one is good but God alone" (Luke 18:19).

Discuss the five ways a man can be Christian in his work (suggested in the reading you have just heard). Relate them to the different kinds of work experienced by those in your group—whether it be work in college, school, the armed services, on-the-job training, part-time work or a full-time career.

Prayer:

O Lord, bless all our work.

Give us the courage to speak with conviction in any difficult situation that may arise, but let us not be discouraged by failure. Let us always remember that we are not perfect.

Help us to serve our neighbor on the job, through the name of Jesus Christ, who did this too and taught us to follow him. Amen.

5. POVERTY? SURVIVAL OF THE FITTEST, YOU KNOW!

Scripture: Jas. 2:15-17, NEB

"Suppose a brother or a sister is in rags with not enough food for the day, and one of you says, 'Good luck to you, keep yourselves warm, and have plenty to eat', but does nothing to supply their bodily needs, what is the good of that? So with faith; if it does not lead to action, it is in itself a lifeless thing."

Reading:

Americans are a virile independent people, descendents of those who had the courage to leave impossible situations in another country and start afresh with only their wits and a pair of bare hands. We like to remind ourselves of this heritage, and many a public speech today includes the line, "God helps them that help themselves." The words are usually spoken in a quoting-from-the-Bible tone of voice, but they were said by Benjamin Franklin, and applied to a totally different America than the one we know today. However, the feeling still lingers that if a man is poor, it is due to lack of effort on his part.

The predicament of the increasing number of unemployed has led to many articles on the subject and to anti-poverty legislation. This in turn has resulted in a strong reaction from many people. According to a Gallup poll, taken in 1964, 33 percent of the nation believes that poverty is caused by lack of effort; 29 percent believes it is due to circumstances; and 32 percent believes it is due to a mixture of circumstances and lack of effort.[10]

In response to an article in the *Saturday Evening Post*, one woman wrote to the editor:

"Nowhere in this article dealing with America's poor was there any mention made of the iniquity of the burden placed by these highly prolific but unproductive members of our society on the middle class tax-payer—the one who limits his family, handles his hard earned money with care and lives within his means."[11]

Another wrote:

"What is your magazine trying to do—undermine our peace of mind with socialist or big-government propaganda? Everyone knows that in a capitalist economy where everyone follows his own profit-making motive, all society will automatically benefit. It is the duty of our business leaders to automate for higher profits. If a few million inefficient people don't fit, well—survival of the fittest you know."[12]

Suggestions for Discussion and Action:

You might want to take a poll of your own on the cause of poverty. (In addition to the figures you have just heard, 6 percent had no opinion. Isn't this a subject every American should have thought about sufficiently to have formed an opinion? Or, at least, every Christian?) After the poll discuss the subject thoroughly, especially the circumstances that have caused poverty. How have they changed since Benjamin Franklin's day? Are these changes due more to natural or to man-made circumstances? What has been done recently in the War on Poverty? Are you aware of the VISTA program?

Read the selected scripture again and suggest everyone listen to it with reference to your discussion. (They seem to have had this problem in the day of James too!)

You may want to have a further discussion of this subject, by inviting an expert or a panel of people qualified to show the point of view of the social worker, the doctor, the employer, the church worker among the poor, the government employment agent, and the politician.

It is to be hoped that you will finish, not with a clearer picture of black and white, but a deeper understanding of several shades of gray. (See also some of the topics in Chapter II.)

What can you do in the way of action? This will depend on the degree of unemployment in your area. Talk to your pastor, and the public health nurse, and, also, consider action in a wider area.

Prayer:

"O God, our Heavenly Father, we beseech Thee to hear us on behalf of . . . all who are poor, and broken and oppressed. For all whose labour is without hope; for all whose labour is without honour. For all whose labour is without interest. For those who have too little leisure. For those who are underpaid. We pray for . . . those who cannot find work, for those who have no home. For all prisoners and outcasts. For all who are sick, hungry, or destitute. We pray O Father, for all men everywhere, that it may please Thee to comfort, sustain, protect and support these, and all others for whom we desire to pray, through Jesus Christ our Lord. Amen." [13]

6. MONEY, MONEY, MONEY!

Scripture: Luke 12:15-21 ("The rich . . . fool.")

Reading:

There was a certain man who wrote to the editor of the *Wall Street Journal:*

"In regard to your editorial of June 1, 'The Pursuit of Unhappiness,' which quotes Adlai Stevenson as saying that we Americans have no purpose in life, I wish to mention the following: I earned a good part of my college expenses firing a locomotive on the Erie Railroad. I have reared and college-educated my four children. I have made a contribution to the future education of my seven grandchildren. I have built a fair-sized competence. I contributed substantially 10% of what income is left after state and federal taxes to my church and other charitable organizations. I am living happily with the bride I took 39 years ago. I will complete, next year, forty years of service to my company. (Excepting a leave of absence to serve in the Air Force in World War II.) Now that I own a twin-screw cabin cruiser with hot and cold running water and a shower bath (after 40 years of damned hard work) comes Mr. Adlai Stevenson to tell me I should sink my boat, buy a pair of water wings, and thus give myself a purpose in life." [14]

"There was another man of great wealth, who had also come by it the hard way. He had a feeling of acute responsibility that . . . [his money] should do as much good as possible. He gave to his church, too, and then spent many hours trying to find out who needed financial help. A certain family had its fuel bill for the winter paid before the husband came home from hospital; a gifted boy was able to go to college for four years; innumerable boxes of groceries were delivered at Thanksgiving time; in fact, no one will ever know exactly how many people were helped, or causes and organizations supported. This certain man was so busy trying to find the best way to spend his money that he would have had no time to sail a yacht, had he bought one." [15]

Suggestions for Discussion and Action:

We often hear of the sacrifice made by those who have very little money, and yet are determined to give, but we rarely hear anything about the decisions made by millionaires—except with caustic comment about income tax deductions. Yet the more a man earns, the harder it is to spend it wisely and responsibly.

What does the church have to say about the way a man should spend his money? With various oblique approaches it indicates that he should *give to his church* for the good of his soul, for foreign missions, new robes for the choir, etcetera, etcetera, etcetera (if it is a comfortable church). There is little leadership as to how he should spend it outside in the world.

As the church seeks to renew itself today, it is reexamining Christian giving. Churches are exempt from taxation, yet some now feel that this is wrong, and that the law should be changed. Some have made the change voluntarily by setting aside the sum they would have paid in taxes, and used it for some specific cause.

Many individuals, as they seek a greater spiritual discipline, seek an economic one too. Each has to work out his own, but he discusses the problem with others and joins them in an actual vow to set aside a certain percentage of his income. (See information on the Iona Community; Taizé; Kirkridge; the Church of our Saviour, Washington, D.C., etc.)

Instead of reading the selected scripture again, read Matt. 6:1-4 ("Do not let your left hand know what your right hand is doing"). This is difficult for us all. We have a gold star complex and want to get credit for what we do. Relate this passage with the reading about the two men and the points raised above.

Why do we give? (Whether it be money, gifts, or assistance.)

How does anyone decide what should be spent on a local church? Don't make the mistake of going too far in the opposite direction, if you are comfortable. After all, a church has normal operational expenses, and no charge is ever made for services rendered! We do not expect a store to give us a free pair of shoes, but we expect the church to give us free voice lessons if we sing in the choir! Ask your pastor to explain the church budget to you, and find out how many services are done by volunteers, such as janitor work, repairs, and yard work. If your group were to volunteer to do some of this maintenance work, could you guarantee the same standard of efficiency and reliability as the paid worker?

Plan a discussion on the use of money as a Christian responsibility.

Prayer:

"Lord, . . . deliver us from both the contempt of money and the over-valuing of it. May we use it with reverence for the enrichment of life, and not its impoverishment. Amen." [16]

7. THE CHURCH AND PR

Scripture: John 12:20-26 ("Sir, we wish to see Jesus.")

Reading: (can be shared between two people)

Today we find the church in industry. The church in *industry?* How? You mean ministers wandering around the machinery in their black robes, giving the workers a spiritual pat on the head? Ridiculous—and dangerous too! Not that? Oh, you mean sermonettes during coffee breaks? No? Well, what place *does* the church have in industry?

If the church is to percolate into all of life, it must go where a man works, too, but the trouble is that the church does not know much about industry, unions, wage disputes, overtime, production, and such matters. But it does know something about Public Relations. In fact, what is evangelism but a form of Public Relations? What is loving thy neighbor but a form of evangelism? After all, a man sees more of his neighbor at the next machine than the one over the back fence at home.

The church comes to industry, not to preach, but to find out what is going on there. It would like those who work there—the salesmen, and executives, and custodians, and clerks, and floor bosses, and office boys, and supervisors—to explain to the church how they work, how they get along with those above, below, and beside them, what they enjoy, and what troubles them into getting ulcers. The church has many questions to ask, and perhaps in turn men and women may have questions to ask the church.

How can this public relations, between the two, take place? Obviously, meetings can be held in the church. There can be panels and films and forums. There can be weekend retreats. These things can be good, but they are apt to draw the white collar crowd, the top brass with theories to expound; and the views of the man with a rag and an oil can are every bit as important, but he is less likely to come. What then?

The church working right in industry—industrial chaplains with no other responsibility, whose congregation may be the Hot Air Plastic Bag Company or Underwood Aviation, Inc. No robes, no collar, no church around the corner. Just an ordained minister who hopes to be able to give the answers to the questions he hopes to be asked. And he doesn't want deep questions like, "What is systematic theology?" Or, "What is the Neo-Orthodox concept of the shape of the liturgy?" He wants to be asked, "What's church all about, anyway?" And, "What is Christ to me?" And, "How can I cope with hating a man who works for me?" And, "Who am I?" and, "How can I stop worrying about getting fired?"

George MacLeod of the Iona Community tells a story of missionaries in China, who put away their Bibles when a famine came and concentrated on serving rice to long lines of starving men. It was disturbing, at first, to find out that about every seventh person, once his bowl was filled, wanted to know about Jesus. The next day a tent was rigged up, with the word "Evangelist" pinned to it. As the questioners came again, to say, " 'Sir, we would see Jesus,' the server brightly pointed to the Evangelist's tent. But without exception the enquirers remonstrated, 'We do not want to hear about Him from the man in the tent but from you who so costingly care.' " [17]

We are a long way from the days when missionaries were welcome in China, but the story still has meaning. It can be seen in action anywhere a Christian serves his fellow men; in a factory, coal mine, East Harlem Protestant Parish, or a plant manufacturing guided missiles. (And what questions might be asked there!)

The public relations campaign of the church has no hard-sell or soft-sell techniques. Perhaps that is why the old hard-sell kind of evangelism does not work today. Nor does the minister who serves in a factory have a quota of conversions to fill. He is there only because he loves his fellow men the way Christ loves them.

Suggestions for Discussion and Action:

Read the scripture again. Isn't that simple line, "Sir, we wish to see Jesus," the one that every man wants to ask, face-to-face, whether he is a Christian or not? We want to know, to be told, to experience, to be challenged, to have faith, and above all, we want to be committed to obey.

Does this mean that face-to-face contact, with questions, is all? Are we to abolish church buildings, and are all our ordained ministers to serve, camouflaged, in factory, store, and office? What do you think?

This is but a new step *alongside* the minister with a congregation in a church. What do you think the next steps should be? (Meetings after work, weekend retreats, Bible study groups, worship together; then participation in public service, the decision to become a member—then out into the world again, a person made new in Christ.)

For further information, about the Kirchentag, see pp. 169-72.

Prayer:

Lord God, we thank thee for the insight and courage of those whom thou has called to lead thy church along a new path, out into the world where Christ waits for all those who are weary and heavy laden. In his name we pray. Amen.

8. TIME OFF—FOR WHAT?

Scripture: Eccl. 3:1-12 ("A time for every matter.")

Reading:

What does a man do with his time? These days there is great interest in what he does with his leisure, as more and more people work shorter hours.

It sounds good, doesn't it?

"Time to do as I please—to sleep late, to go fishing, to get away from a clock!"

Why, then, did a recent article on leisure carry a picture of a husband and wife looking utterly bored and frustrated? He, in unbecoming Bermuda shorts, with his feet up, twiddling his thumbs. She, obviously wondering how she could put up with the man until he went back to work, also twiddling her thumbs. Can it be that people, like school children, welcome the summer vacation but are quite eager to get back to school at the end of it?

Yet, supplying the materials and places for leisure has become a major American business. Do-it-yourself kits boom; water skiing has been replaced by surfing; every car must have its boat trailer; bowling leagues are an elaborate industry; and more and groups of determined people migrate to Europe every summer in search of ready-mixed culture.

It all sounds like the song that said, "Everybody's doing it *now!*" —and maybe that's the trouble. "Everybody" is in the act, and there is nothing original or creative in any of it.

Is there anything original in painting a picture with numbers for each color, or joining a ceramics class to paint a figurine someone else has made? Is there anything original in watching other people play football on TV, or in becoming an expert in knowing the names of all the Green Bay Packers? Is there anything original about camping out in a hut with all the modern conveniences, a garbage can, and a stack of TV dinners?

In all these comfortable activities that go under the name of "leisure" there is no involvement of the individual self. Is this the trouble? Everyone is following a prescribed pattern of behavior, just as if someone rang a bell and said, "Now children, you may all play, and this is how you must do it!"

No child will play to order, and children understand leisure better than we do, for most of their early years are spent in exploring through doing—in touching, seeing, hearing, and making use of the imagination. A thoughtful parent tries to give his child the opportunity to do these things *on his own*. He exposes him to beauty in the outdoors, in art, music, and literature. He arouses his interest in great ideas and teaches him values so that he can discriminate between the true and the imitation. He gives him the opportunity to think on his own, create on his own, and grow in many directions.

If adults followed these same suggestions in their leisure time, they would continue to grow also and develop the particular talents God gave them.

It has been said that those who have explored on their own and searched after the most education are also those who adjust more easily to a long period of inactivity—perhaps, caused by illness or retirement. Faced with the opportunity for leisure all day long, they continue to explore and study, as well as to make use of resources already accumulated within them. Such people are more apt to know the names of the different kinds of birds that come to feed outside their window than the names of the Green Bay Packers. They would rather discuss a book just read then play canasta. Their fellow men may consider them a little odd at times, for they possess enough security and serenity through knowledge of themselves and the world, to not want to do what "everybody" is doing *now!*

There should be no anxiety in leisure, no tension, no pressure. A man should be doing what he feels inclined to do, at the pace he chooses, or he is being influenced by what everybody else is doing.

Where is God in all this? In it all, of course! Robert Lee has said, "To an anxious and troubled generation of Americans faced with the prospect of still greater leisure, the Biblical injunction contained in Psalm 46—'Be still, and know that I am God' really means in its full Biblical setting: 'Cease, stop, relax. . . . Have leisure and know that I am God.'" [18]

Suggestions for Discussion and Action:

The Bible has nothing to say about leisure, for there was little of it—in our sense of the word—among a people who worked from dawn to dusk, but it does speak of the use made of time. Read the selected scripture again, from verses 1-8. Just as there is a rhythm to these lines, so also there seemed to be a rhythm in the lives of these people, and a time for everything.

God created the seventh day for rest, but in our complex world many have to work on that day, while others have different days for rest. If God still spoke of his displeasure with men, through one of his prophets, we can be sure he would "abominate" the use of the words "killing time." But can we be sure that he does not still speak through a prophet, and that we, like the children of Israel, cannot be bothered to listen?

The amount of leisure each person has will vary considerably. Although leisure is becoming a problem, it is not one that affects everyone yet. It runs the gamut from the business chief, or self-employed man who may work very long hours, through those who are able to count on several days off a week, to the unemployed whose life is nothing but enforced leisure.

What does this say to us as Christians who live in the thick of things? Can you take life easy all day long, getting a tan in the backyard, knowing that your neighbor has three children under four and never has a moment of free time? Can you plan your own leisure, knowing that there are others who do not know how to do so, through poor education or lack of recreation facilities?

In other words, do we need to work out a discipline and a rhythm to our hours of leisure with:

A time to read, and a time to play tennis.

A time to sing, and a time to swim.

A time to take the car apart, and a time to cook for the fun of it.

A time to dream, and a time to give to others.

Anyone in your group who has a little time to give to others, and does not know what to do with it should read *all* of Chapter IX!

Prayer:

"This is the day which the Lord has made;
let us rejoice and be glad in it" (Ps. 118:24).

ADDITIONAL WORSHIP RESOURCES

Scripture:

Gen. 1:26–2:3 ("God saw everything he had made.")

Gen. 2:4-15 ("God put man in the garden of Eden to till and keep it.")

Exod. 20:8-11 ("Six days you shall labor.")

Ps. 8 ("The work of thy fingers.")

Ps. 104:1, 14-24 ("Plants for man to cultivate.")

Isa. 58:10-12 ("Satisfy the desire of the afflicted.")

Matt. 11:28-30 ("Come . . . all who labor and are heavy-laden.")

Matt. 20:1-16 ("The kingdom of heaven is like a householder.")

Matt. 25:31-40 ("As you did it to one of the least of these.")

Mark 6:1-6 ("Is not this the carpenter?")

John 15:1-5 ("I am the true vine; . . . apart from me you can do nothing.")

I Cor. 3:5-9 ("God gave the growth.")
I Cor. 9:7-10 ("Who serves as a soldier at his own expense?")
I Cor. 10:31 ("Do all to the glory of God.")
Phil. 4:10-13 ("I can do all things in him.")
Eph. 6:5-9 ("Be obedient to . . . earthly masters.")
Col. 3:23-24 ("Whatever your task, work heartily.")
I Thess. 4:9-12 ("Aspire . . . to work.")
I Thess. 5:12-18 ("Help the weak.")
Selections from Proverbs, for calls to worship or to use antiphonally 6:6-11; 10:5; 12:11; 12:27; 13:11; 14:23; 21:5; 27:23; 28:19.

Prayers:

We pray:
"That we may prepare ourselves as thoroughly as possible for getting work.

That we may share work as we are able.

That we may really sympathize with the unemployed.

That we may inform ourselves about labor conditions and work for the passage of fair labor laws.

That we may avoid the feeling that the world owes us a living.

That we may keep our faith in God even if we cannot find work." [19]

"Teach us, good Lord, to serve Thee as Thou deservest:
To give and not to count the cost;
To fight and not to heed the wounds;
To strive and not to seek for rest;
To labor and not to ask for reward,
Saving the knowledge that we do Thy will." [20]

Lord, we look at the beauty of the world you continue to create; the wing of a bird, the sea, a tree in the wind, the convolutions of a shell. These things are wonderful indeed. We look at the hands you have given us, and wonderful are the things they can do. Sometimes we take for granted. Help us to see them afresh as instruments with which we can create the wonderful and the beautiful too, and all to the glory of thy name. Amen.

Hymns:

    We Thank Thee, Lord, Thy Paths of Service Lead
    O Son of Man, Thou Madest Known
    O Master, Let Me Walk with Thee
    Lord God of Hosts, Whose Purpose Never Swerving
    We Plough the Fields and Scatter
    Believe Not Those Who Say the Upward Path Is Smooth
    Go, Labor On
    God of the Nations, Hear Our Call
    O Master Workman of the Race

chapter VI

LIVING OUT ON A LIMB

1. IS THERE A TIME OF RELIGIOUS HIBERNATION?

Scripture: II Pet. 1:2-9, 3:15-18 ("Supplement . . . knowledge
with self-control.")

Reading:

When young people leave home for the first time, they are very
apt to go into religious hibernation. No matter whether they go
to college, take a job, enlist in the Marines, or even get married,
they very naturally want to leave the apron strings of childhood
behind them and become thinking, deciding adults on their own.
Many do not throw religion overboard completely. They just want
it out of the way for a few years, in hibernation. But hibernation is
a deep sleep. Just at the time when the new adult is forging out his
own ideas and beliefs about everything religion *should* be included.

If he has come from a background which makes him feel that
churchgoing is a form of celestial insurance policy, just in case
there *is* a God, or that God is a *Good Thing*—along with vitamins,
and dental checkups—it is even more of a pity if he puts his re-

ligion to sleep, for perhaps it is not what he decided it was at all!

The students on an eastern campus were startled one day when a minister, complete with clerical collar, announced that he was an atheist! A Christian atheist he called himself.

What did he mean? He defined an atheist as "a person who has some concept or idea of God *in which* (*or in whom*) *he doesn't believe.*" He said, "The important fact for you to remember is that every atheist has an idea of God, for if he didn't, there wouldn't be anything for him to be against." [1]

This minister—whose name is Robert Montgomery—often asks a student to clue him in on the God in whom he does not believe, and after the student has done so, shakes him by the hand as a fellow atheist, for he doesn't believe in that kind of God either!

You have probably heard about Bishop J. A. T. Robinson's book *Honest to God.* [2] It shocked many more people *outside* of the church than in it when he debunked the idea of a God "up there," "an old man in the sky." They had decided that with the probing of man into outer space, with rockets and telescopes and possible trips to the moon, there could be no God up there or they would have discovered him by now. They thought that it was they who had rejected the up-there idea of God, and were startled to find that most church people had discarded it many years ago and had an utterly different concept of God.

The true and living God is present no matter how people try to imagine him. Leslie Weatherhead has pointed out that you cannot put a tape measure round God, and decide that "this is what he is." Exploration into space makes God seem even greater, and our knowledge of him even more inconclusive.

There is nothing particularly daring in putting God into hibernation. It is much more daring—and responsible—to go out on a limb and find him, and find Jesus Christ. It means doing a great deal of listening—not to people who say, "This is what you should believe," but to those willing to go out on a limb also and say, "This is what I believe, and why."

It may help us to regain our perspective if we think of the Russian child who asked, " 'Mother, we don't believe in God, do we?'

To which his mother replied, 'Of course not, child.' Then: 'Mother, does God know we don't believe in him?' " [3]

Suggestions for Discussion and Action:

Read the scripture again. You will notice that even in the early church there were people who had odd ideas, who made snap decisions, and did not examine thoroughly the way to come to "the knowledge of our Lord Jesus Christ" (II Pet. 1:8).

Dr. Weatherhead has said, "Christianity, to me, is a way of life. A Christian is someone who believes that Christ's Way is the supreme way of life, who tries to follow it and who tries to respond to the demands of life in a Christ-like spirit."

What is Christ's way? What does he demand?

The following scripture may be helpful: Matt. 7:7-12; 22:34-39; John 11:17-27; 13:1-15; 14:5-17; II Cor. 5:16-20. Take time to study these passages, as if for the first time, but beware of hibernating in Bible study! Study must be followed by action, by service (John 13:13-15). Sometimes the two need to be related together before finding a mature faith in God through Jesus Christ. Some form of serving the real needs of living people can make the words in the Bible come alive.

Prayer:

O Lord God, waken us into an awareness that there is a Christian way of life and that we may not have found it yet. Help us to prick our present beliefs and see if they are real. Help us not only to discard any wrong thinking, but to search until we can replace the void with a new faith in thee through Jesus Christ. And above all, help us to study thy Word in the Bible until that Word finds us. Amen.

2. "CHRISTIANS" WHO PLAY IT COOL

Scripture: Matt. 16:13-17 ("You are the Christ.")

Reading:

Many Americans who call themselves Christians today are inclined to be quiet about their faith, to play it down, to act embarrassed when they see someone else getting emotional about their beliefs. In other words, they either lack conviction or are "chicken."

Perhaps this is because Christianity has become diluted and watered down. People do not seem to care much about the beliefs of the different denominations. When they move to a new community, they choose a church that seems to fit their social status, or perhaps one with a new building, a friendly minister, or a good Sunday school. It is easy to get a letter of transfer that changes one from a Methodist to a Lutheran, or from a Congregationalist to a Presbyterian. Words like "conversion" or "commitment" are rarely heard, except in the lower-income-bracket churches, which no one notices anyway. The "in" people play it cool, with a light touch of cynicism.

Yet there is a great deal of activity in most of today's churches —what Peter Berger, in the title of his book, has called *The Noise of Solemn Assemblies* [4] (taken from the words of God to his wayward people in the book of Amos). There is nothing new in this casual approach, this busyness with things God does not require. They are part of the ebb and flow of the behavior of God's people down through the centuries, and at the moment we seem to be at a very low ebb. Perhaps the tide will turn if we are willing to learn again the meaning of the word "conversion."

Anyway, just what *is* conversion?

Conversion is something that happens outside of ourselves. "It tells us that the God who created the distant nebulae, the God who is other than anything we can imagine, has come to us. . . . The eyes of the Christian faith look not inward into itself but outward towards this man Jesus, of whom the New Testament speaks and who asked the question of His early followers: 'Who do you say that I am?' Conversion to the Christian faith is the answer to this question, the one once given by Simon Peter—the stupendous affirmation that the man asking the question is the Christ, the Savior." [5]

The tragedy of the "Christian" who plays it cool is that he is never listening, never searching. He is quite happy as he is, and totally unaware that it is preposterous for him to call himself a Christian.

Do we have the courage to hope that we may be converted?

Suggestions for Discussion and Action:

Read the scripture again. Can we answer as Peter did, or is our faith a secondhand affair? Find out what meanings those in your group place on the word "conversion."

Bring up the old gospel-tent style of conversion, the campfire experiences, and the mass rallies—if no one else mentions them. To what degree are our emotions involved, and to what extent should we be guided by them?

Why are we afraid to talk about these things? Where and when is the best place to start?

Have we become lukewarm and apathetic? Read Rev. 3:15-22. They are words addressed to the church in Laodicea. Could they be addressed to us too?

Do you feel that the church needs to recover a discipline among its members? Should there be stricter requirements before membership, at the time of a transfer, and throughout life after membership? Apparently some churches feel this is needed. Check the end of this chapter. Instead of the usual additional prayers, you will find a few of the new "disciplines" some churches have drawn up. Notice that they are quite different from the gold-star-for-good-behavior charts that have so little meaning.

Prayer:

O Lord, we know that our sickness is our softness. "We are destroyed by our preference for the trivial, our fear of the serious. We must learn to read our Bibles. . . . We must learn to pray, to stretch our mental and spiritual muscles. We must seek the inner witness and the personal knowledge of God as if it were the most important things in life," [6] and we know it is. Amen.

3. SEXPLOSION

Scripture: I Cor. 13:4-7 ("Love does not insist on its own way.")

Reading:

"Some of the more backward countries in the world are suffering from a population explosion. One of the more advanced countries in the world, the United States, is suffering from *sexplosion*—sexploitation being the most popular form of conspicuous consumption in the affluent society.

"The sexplosion has two obvious features. One might be labeled simply as sex on the loose. It is characterized by the discarding of many historic moral restraints, great indulgence in premarital sexual intercourse, earlier marriages, more unwanted babies, more frequent resort to adoption agencies. Among emancipated spirits this complex of activities is generally referred to as the 'new freedom.' . . .

"When we turn away from the frauds and the illusions to the realities of the present scene, one fact stands out: young people today are losing control of their lives. They are having babies when they don't want them. They are getting married before they really want to. They are taking jobs before they are adequately prepared for them. And this is the 'new freedom'! But freedom is precisely what is being lost. There is pathos in the life of anyone who has cheated himself of the freedom really to choose to get married, to choose to have a baby, to choose to take a job. . . .

"With the growth of realism in the . . . younger generation, perhaps even their teachers will begin to rediscover that many of the so-called 'traditional controls' are deeply rooted in the common sense of the race. In the outcome there should be at least three ingredients: (1) a newly achieved frankness about sex and love, not merely grounded in science, but shored up by great traditions of value in literature, religion and ethics; (2) an unequivocal affirmation that sex belongs to the 'whole man,' that it cannot be separated, without incurring natural penalties, from love, honor, duty, loyalty, sacrifice, 'for better for worse, for richer for poorer, in sickness and in health'; (3) a fresh understanding of the fact that sex, far from being merely personal, is irretrievably social in its significance—and that its relationship to family and to children, to community and to country, and to the several arts and sciences of man are a part of the privileges and responsibilities into which we enter when we share in it." [7]

Suggestions for Discussion and Action:

There have been too many frank talks on sex to youth groups; too many panel discussions led by a doctor or a nurse; too much accent on the scientific and biological; too many churches who pride themselves on being progressive in doing so and have not realized they are emphasizing only one side of the question.

Present this view and have a time for discussion of it in light of the reading just heard. Read the selected scripture again and add it to the discussion. What does it say to the present sex situation?

Suggest an informal group discussion in the near future to which you would invite: a couple who married during high school; a couple who married during college and "she" is working to put "him" through; a couple who had to give up plans for higher education because they married after graduating from high school; and a couple who "had" to get married. Open the discussion by reading the second paragraph of the reading you have just heard and ask those invited to comment on it. Be careful that you do not at any time give the impression you are asking for a confessional beginning, "We made a mistake." This is a time for evaluation, question, and answer—never criticism or judgment.

You may want to include discussion of freedom versus restraint.

What does youth of today think of the "new freedom"? What does all this have to do with the church?

Prayer:

O Lord, we thank you for the inexpressible joy that can be known by two people who love each other. Teach us to be patient and kind. Give us integrity and honesty and the capacity to love as we are loved. Grant us the courage to face the freedom of these days with decisions that will protect the lives of those we love, rather than suiting our own desires. In all things let us remember that you first loved us and gave us your own son, Jesus Christ, in whose name we pray. Amen.

4. THE TEN COMMANDMENTS TODAY

Scripture: Matt. 22:34-40 ("The great commandment.")

Reading:

(Three readers: the first will read quite fast in a conversational tone; the second will read at a more moderate speed; the third will read the scripture slowly and carefully.)

First Reader: I saw an amusing cartoon in a magazine the other day. It showed figures dancing along carrying placards that read, "God is good for you!" "Religion can be fun!" and "Join now, and be saved later!"

Second Reader: Funny, but with a lot of truth in it. How seriously do we take our membership in the church? Do we try to discipline our lives and follow the precepts of Jesus Christ? Do we obey the Ten Commandments?

Third Reader: Deut. 5:1-3, 6-7.

First Reader: But that's absurd! People don't worship a collection of gods any more. I mean, this refers to pagan practices, to

142

the gods of the Greeks or the Egyptians, invented out of fear and superstition.

Second Reader: And yet—although we still talk about him a lot —do we perhaps worship no God at all? Do we throw him away at the same time that we outgrow Santa Claus and the Easter Bunny? When I look at a rainbow or a rose, at the hand of an old man or the fingernails of a new baby, then I know there must be a God.

Third Reader: Deut. 5:8.

First Reader: Well, all *that* means is that you can't see God, and frankly, I won't believe in something I can't see. I think man has progressed far beyond this sort of thing. A man who can orbit the earth, transplant an eye, and invent an IBM machine is self-sufficient.

Second Reader: I think you are admitting that man still does worship graven images! He worships his rocket, his surgical skill, his computer, and even himself. Don't forget, it was God who gave man the brain to work out these things and the ability to communicate ideas with others. Surely we should glorify God for them and not ourselves?

Third Reader: Deut. 5:11.

First Reader: Now I ask you! People swear all the time and it doesn't mean a thing! It's just a figure of speech. When I say "Good God," I don't refer to the goodness of God, I refer to. . . .

Second Reader: Yes, just what *do* you refer to? (pause)

Third Reader: Deut. 5:12-14.

First Reader: This is, of course, very interesting from an ethnological point of view, for it depicts forms of living among the ancient Hebrews. But I don't have an ox, or an ass, and I don't believe you have a maid-servant. As for laboring six days, we are more enlightened and have a forty-hour week. In fact, we insist on periods of rest all through the day—coffee breaks, noon hour, etc.

Second Reader: Working conditions *are* different, and we don't have that strict Sunday our grandparents knew. That wasn't right either. I think Sunday should first of all include the attendance of a service of worship. Then it should be a day of rest and recreation.

Third Reader: Deut. 5:16.

First Reader: This is out of date too! People don't grovel before their parents any more. The obedient family went out with *Life with Father,* and talk of "togetherness" won't bring it back. The family is purely a status symbol.

Second Reader: It happens to be the way God planned that children should be cared for till they were capable of living on their own. We know our parents make mistakes, just like we do. It's not till we realize that they love us "no matter what," that we come to love them "no matter what" too, and know they are trying to help us to become mature adults. For this, we honor them.

Third Reader: Deut. 5:17.

First Reader: Well, I agree with this one, of course.

Second Reader: Yes. Yet, I wonder if it does not mean hurting people in *any* way. Ridiculing, ignoring, being angry. Have you never heard someone say, "He just killed my soul!" or, "I could have died"? With a really vicious attack on someone you do cause them to die a little.

Third Reader: Deut. 5:18.

First Reader: Another archaic one!

Second Reader: Jesus put a very different interpretation on that word. He taught that it even included thinking about adultery. Maybe today it should even include the enjoyment of jokes about sex, or setting a low standard in books we read and movies we see.

Third Reader: Deut. 5:19.

First Reader: Well, I know *I'm* not a thief!

Second Reader: Oh? I wish I could say the same thing! There was that time I cribbed someone else's idea in a term paper; the time the candy machine stuck, and we all got free candy—but was it *really* free? Did you always give the change back to your mother when she forgot to ask for it?

Third Reader: Deut. 5:20.

First Reader: What on earth is "false witness"?

Second Reader: Plain, ordinary, spiteful gossip, gingered up a little to delight the listener and belittle the subject of the gossip.

Third Reader: Deut. 5:21.

Third Reader: Another reference to ancient days! When a man's wealth was seen visibly in his goods and chattels.

Second Reader: Have you never known envy? I have. I envy George's Alfa Romeo. I wish I had hair like Mary. I wish I could go steady with Mike, but Jean is, and I almost hate her for it. Yet, I know God has given me many things, and for these I thank him.

Third Reader: Deut. 6:5.

Second Reader: Jesus added to this, "And you shall love your neighbor as yourself." Believing and keeping these two commandments, it would be impossible not to keep the others!

Suggestions for Discussion and Action:

You will need advance preparation for the use of this topic, and it may require two sessions.

The dialogue would probably be frustrating, if it were used as it is printed. Try breaking it after the second reader has spoken, every time, and give everyone in your group a chance to argue with both the first and second readers. Do not let each discussion become too prolonged, so that the overall survey of the Ten Commandments is lost. To avoid this, you could leave it to the third reader to continue with the next Commandment when sufficient time has been allowed. You might also want to have someone give a brief resumé of the historical setting of the Commandments within the Old Testament, perhaps at the beginning. (*The Abingdon Bible Commentary*[8] would be a useful resource here.) The second reader might also like to look through Chapter IX for examples of practical action which would make the Commandments more relevant to today.

Before reading the prayer below, discuss it, too, with your group. Perhaps the most well-known of the prayers of general confession, it was written many years ago and is still used, not just because it is part of the traditional liturgy of the church, but because it still seems relevant to every generation. However, some of the words (such as "devices" and "godly"), have a different meaning today, and some explanation will make them more understandable. Here again, your first and second reader might be prepared beforehand to do this.

Prayer: (to be said in unison.)

"Almighty and most merciful Father; We have erred and strayed from Thy ways like lost sheep. We have followed too much the devices and desires of our own hearts. We have offended against Thy holy laws. We have left undone those things which we ought to have done; And we have done those things which we ought not to have done; And there is no health in us. But Thou, O Lord, have mercy upon us, miserable offenders. Spare Thou, those O God, who confess their faults. Restore Thou those who are penitent; According to Thy promises declared unto mankind in Christ Jesus our Lord. And grant, O most merciful Father, for His sake; That we may hereafter live a godly, righteous, and sober life; To the glory of Thy holy name. Amen." [9]

5. THOU SHALT GET BY WITH IT

Scripture: I John 1:5-10 ("If we say we have no sin, we deceive ourselves.")

Reading:

A cynic has suggested that the Ten Commandments should be brought up to date by the addition of an eleventh one, "Thou shalt get by with it." In other words it doesn't matter what you do, so long as you are smart enough to avoid getting punished or caught.

People are probably no more inclined to disobey the laws of society today than they were a hundred years ago. They are just more frank about admitting it, for under the current cult of permissiveness it is easier to "get by with it," and any punishment is apt to be watered down with the application of sympathetic psychology. (It was not really your fault. You had a compulsion to cheat because someone punished your mother unfairly when she was in the kindergarten, and she has wanted to get back at authority ever since!)

Increased knowledge of psychology has led to a more compassionate understanding of why people break laws and rules, but at times this has been overdone. There must be some authority in any civilized society, and authority must be upheld by law with known penalties for offenses against it.

The pendulum swings between "spare the rod" and "use the rod." Probably, today's young adults will insist in stricter law enforcement when they become leaders of society. They may want it, or they may be forced into it.

If you are in any doubt about this permissiveness, listen to a few of the common expressions of our times.

"You can't change human nature."

"Nobody is *that* good."

"So what?"

"Everybody does it."

"If you don't look out for yourself, no one else will."

"You have to be practical and realistic."

"If you can't lick 'em, join 'em."

"You have to beat the racket."

"Owning up? That's Mickey Mouse stuff!"

It is hard to have the courage of one's convictions, these days.

Cynical laughter has a bite to it, and the brave ones can suddenly find they are alone or about to be thrown to the lions. Incidentally, when Christians were *literally* thrown to the lions, it was not because they annoyed the authorities by sounding off about their beliefs, but because they would not do what everyone else was doing and worship the current emperor as divine. Can't you imagine many a noble Roman using expressions quite similar to the ones you have just heard. "No, I don't believe old Nero is a god either, but it's smart to be realistic about it. So it's a lie when I go to the temple to honor him? Everyone else is doing it. Who cares, anyway?"

Some of the more demoralizing situations in society today, are those which are not covered by any law, or for which the law is out-of-date or is not upheld.

Take smoking among minors, as an example. In many states it is illegal for a minor to buy cigarettes or to smoke in certain places. Most people know about the first, but are unaware of the second. In the greatest majority of cases not only does the minor "get by with it," but some parents are hostile toward those who try to enforce the law! And they "get by with it" too! Here is a case where action should be taken to see that the law is enforced or that the law is changed (along with, perhaps, a little education on lung cancer)!

Suggestions for Discussion and Action:

Read the scripture again. The significant line is, of course, "If we say we have no sin we deceive ourselves." This is the problem with the "thou shalt get by with it" kind of thinking, where rules are adjusted to whether you get caught or not (and even when you get caught, but nothing happens). How do the members of your group feel about this easy way of thinking?

What about that word "sin"? Do we say it is old-fashioned, or maybe keep it for the more serious crimes, such as murder? In the end we have to come back to it, for sin is sin, no matter how we try to rationalize it. A Christian is one who knows he will always have to struggle with sin, and we need to make this clear to those outside the church who think we consider ourselves decorated with do-it-yourself halos.

What does the church have to say to the situation of teen-age smoking? (As you discuss this, see if there is a possibility that your group might be able to go out on a limb and do something constructive about it.)

This is probably another situation where the church will be told, "Go back to your prayer meetings and mind your own business!" What *is* the business of the church? Discuss this, hoping that no one will suggest the church rush in with the pursed lips of a Pharisee, muttering, "Thou shalt not smoke," or indicate that nothing you do would make any difference, anyway.

Try to get to the bottom of the situation. Why do these minors flaunt their cigarettes? Is it love of tobacco or a desire to belittle the law? Why do some parents object to its enforcement? Why was it instituted in the first place? If it *is* enforced, will it reduce teen-age smoking? Are law enforcement organizations themselves getting by with it when they look the other way? What can you do to arouse interest in the situation that may lead to its amendment? (Perhaps through your church leaders, school or college council, state representatives, Congressmen, or The American Cancer Society.)

Prayer:

O God, we live in a world of split-level thinking today. Help us to know what we should do and not do. Help us to avoid the easy way out or to give idle criticism upon situations that seem wrong to us. Instead, with your guidance, help us to make right decisions, knowing that each one is different. Amen.

6. THE TIMES CALL FOR MEN WHO DARE

Scripture: Isa. 2:3-4 ("Neither shall they learn war any more.")

Reading:

This was written just after the Cuban crisis, at a time when our country was on the brink of nuclear war. The words mean just as much today, and we need to think about them.

"The times call for men who dare to keep their heads and to refuse to surrender to any expediency the right to be free men in a free society. The crisis calls not for a vain, blatant nationalism but for men who hold in check their fears and their passions, who dare to speak calm, wise words and carry out sane, creative deeds which exemplify freedom, prevent collective hysteria and, please God, lead to peace. The peril must be met by men who publicly honor the truth even when it is painful to us and who, because they love man as well as country, admit their nation's involvement in the sins of the nations. We must not abandon the ancient dream of a just, free and peaceful society for all men—a dream entrusted to us for ourselves and for all peoples. In cold or hot war we must think thoughts, speak words and perform deeds which keep that faith alive—no matter what the cost.

"The struggle to save the soul and the integrity of the nation and the struggle for peace and justice in the world are not two struggles, waged alternately, but one struggle which never ends. It has not been adjourned 'for the duration' of the present crisis and will not be, no matter how long the crisis lasts. Consequently no respite on reason, no moratorium on morality or mercy, no truce on truth, no jettisoning of justice may be tolerated. Until God's judgment is suspended, we are all accountable to him." [10]

Suggestions for Discussion and Action:

Read the scripture again. Have we, in this age of threatening each other with nuclear weapons, given up all hope of lasting peace? These words of Isaiah sound almost too good to be true.

We have always had a strange idea, in time of war, that God must be on our side; therefore, we must be right, and it must be a Holy War. We even pray that he will help us beat our enemies. Now that there is no "hot" war in progress we have made friends with the Japanese and the Germans again, all of us trying to make up for the harm we did to each other. Confusing, isn't it?

How do *you* think the church should work toward peace? Should it be pacifist or militant?

Here are two sides of the picture.

Should the church work for all-out pacifism—the goal being that the major powers would agree to stop the arms race? This would be a calculated risk, but is it one Christians should be prepared to take? The money spent on this race could be diverted toward rehabilitating the hungry in the world or tackling the problem of poverty in this country.

On the other hand, if we did throw down our arms the "enemy" would then be free to walk all over us, and pacifism would be defeated too. How should we interpret Jesus' command that we love our enemy and turn the other cheek? Think of the story of the Good Samaritan. If the thieves had returned to kill the injured man, would the Good Samaritan have stood to one side and let them do so? Is that showing love for one's neighbor? Jesus himself chose to read this passage from Isaiah:

"The Spirit of the Lord is upon me,

because he has anointed me to preach good news to the poor.

He has sent me to proclaim release to the captives

and recovering of sight to the blind,

to set at liberty those who are oppressed,

to proclaim the acceptable year of the Lord" (Luke 4:18-19).

Does the church feel it must support the means by which the weak can be defended from attack or privation?

What do you think?

Dietrich Bonhoeffer had to make a terrible decision a few years before he was killed by the Nazis. He was asked to join a conspiracy to destroy Hitler and his followers. Knowing the evil forces let loose by that regime, and its threat to the free world, he came to the conclusion that there are times when a man has to sin in order to overcome evil. Luther called it, "To sin boldly."

The subject of world peace is not one to be put aside as the responsibility of someone else. We need to "think boldly" about war, about the problems of pacifism, and the dangers of too much blind patriotism. Sometimes it takes more courage to stand out as a pacifist, than to join the army and learn how to kill.

See Chapter IX for the addresses of the Fellowship of Reconciliation and the Friends Service Committee—both peace organizations. In the same chapter you will also find details about the reconciliation movement by German youth.

You might want to end by considering these lines:

> "Onward Christian Soldiers,
> Each to war resigned;
> With the Cross of Jesus,
> Vaguely kept in mind." [11]

Prayer:

O Lord God, who has created this wonderful world in which we live and who knows all things, we are helpless as we try to find the way of peace, proclaimed by your son, Jesus Christ. Show us the path we should take, renew our strength so that we may mount up with wings as eagles and take our place, prepared to lead the coming generation toward peace for all men. Grant us the conviction that will bring courage to others. We pray in the name of Jesus, knowing that without you, all our work will be in vain. Amen.

7. GOD'S FIREWEED

Scripture: Isa. 35:1-4 ("The desert shall rejoice and blossom.")

Reading:

There is a plant called rosebay willow herb or fireweed. It grows in the most unlikely places. Its flowers can be seen among the ruins of a building blackened by fire or on the walls of a derelict house. Its cheerful color was a symbol of the renewal of life, among the wilderness of rubble that followed the air raids of World War II, and it gave hope to many of the homeless.

Just as fireweed appears in the most heartbreaking places and seems to thrive without any nourishment, so also have there always been men who appear in heartbreaking situations and through sheer courage and commitment to God bring hope and light to others. We should call them "God's fireweed."

They are men who see visions and dream dreams, as Joel said. Men who dare to try something utterly different because they feel impelled by God to do so and who usually get the criticism they expect from the organized church. These men are not a part of the past. They are scattered throughout the world today and always will be.

There is *Father Borrelli,* a Roman Catholic, who opened the House of Urchins for the utterly desolate children of Naples who slept in the streets. There is *William Stringfellow,* an Episcopalian layman and a brilliant lawyer, who could have lived in comfort anywhere but chose to open his office in East Harlem and help the Puerto Ricans and Negroes in one of the saddest places in America today.

There is *Pastor Rolf Boiten* who works in the prostitution district of Amsterdam and who has a cabaret on the first floor of his house where sailors and young people can dance, talk, and meet girls from a wholesome background. And there is *Canon Ernest Southcott* who reached out to people who never came to his church, by celebrating Holy Communion on the kitchen table in ordinary homes before the men went to work in the morning. There are *William* and *Gwen Mellon* who spent two million dollars of their own money to start a hospital in a remote jungle on Haiti, and they obtained medical degrees and laboratory training so that they could work there themselves.

There is *James Meredith,* who must have had tremendous self-control and courage to endure what happened to him when he enrolled as the first Negro student at the University of Mississippi, with his every movement and expression being watched by the whole world. Then there were the white students who worked in that same state, one troubled summer, and who stayed there although three of them were murdered.

There is *Pierre Teilhard de Chardin,* the Jesuit priest and paleontologist, who, although he died in 1955, still flickers like fireweed all through the world. Severely disciplined by his church, he saw none of his books in print—for none were allowed to be published until after his death. In them, he tried to reconcile science and religion. This caused great controversy in his church —controversy like a breath of fresh air in a dusty room.

There is *George MacLeod,* of the Church of Scotland, who founded the Iona Community and led the way in making the church realize that it must minister to men where they work and that work is centered in worship. There is *Reinhold von Thadden,* a layman, who founded the tremendous Lay Congress called the Kirchentag, when as many as 350,000 Germans will assemble together, although the German church was about dead after the war.

There is *Tullio Vinay,* who founded Agape, the Waldensian Ecumenical Youth Center in the Italian Alps. Such was the spirit of Christian love—agape—that young people from countries that had been on opposite sides during World War II could meet and talk together. Then Pastor Vinay went to Sicily, where people live in terror under the gangster Maffia. He brought with him a team of teachers, social workers, agricultural experts, doctors, and pastors to help the *whole* life of a people who feel that the world has turned its back on them. He has said, "The Church does not exist to save itself, but to give itself in love and service for those for whom Christ died."

The fireweed can remind us that God works in every corner of the world. When people have given up, he is there, reviving them again. Not with the flourish of organs and the scent of potted lilies, but like a small pink flower in a crack in a wall.

Suggestions for Discussion and Action:

Read the scripture again, the whole chapter, if possible.

Many books and magazines will carry more information about these men. You may want to find out more detail about one of them, or about others not mentioned.

Do you feel that pioneer work such as this is a branch of the church (or denomination to which each man belongs), or is it a part of the organized church, with the same value as the work of a local church?

Why did these men act as they did? What reasons, based on the Word of God, might they have had for striking out on their own? Were they doing what the church had neglected to do?

How can we decide whether new ventures by individuals are a genuine shoot of the church, inspired by God, or just "way out" and "wild"?

Can you, as a group, within your own situation, honestly say that you have the courage to strike out on your own when the need to do so arises? Or, what is more important, can you think of actual situations where you *have* acted, or have failed to act? What was the element of difficulty?

Prayer:

O God, we give thanks for the knowledge that, even today, you still lead men into adventures of faith in new ways and in new places. We give thanks, also, for their abilities to listen, see, and do. Give us, we pray, the sense to know the truth as it is in Christ, and kindle in us some small spark of courage that will help us to know your will and do it. Amen.

8. THE CHURCH OF THE SAVIOUR, WASHINGTON, D.C.

Scripture: II Cor. 5:16-20 ("If any one is in Christ, he is a new creation.")

Reading:

The Church of the Saviour in Washington, D.C. has dared to become what its members feel a church should really be. It does not have what we would call a "proper" church building at all. Instead, there is a large house, called "Headquarters," with a library, guest rooms, kitchen, office, etc. Nor does its coffee shop, "The Potter's House," have any normal "churchiness" about it either.

The church is its members.

Most of us today see the church as it is in the rhyme:

> "Here is the church, and here is the steeple;
> Open the door and look at the people."

We expect a building that can be recognized as a church (even though steeples have gone out of fashion). We expect a pulpit, and pews, and windows that are different in some way from those in an ordinary house. But why? There was nothing like this in the New Testament. Christians met in each other's houses, often with a meal around a table—far different from our Communion table— and the church of God—say, in Corinth—was a group of *people*.

The totally different thing about the Church of the Saviour is not so much that it has no usual church building, but that it has very rigid requirements for membership. It actually dares to send people away, not because they are unworthy, or unsuitable, or the wrong color, but because they are unwilling to accept these requirements.

The congregation feels that it is a very serious matter for any one to make his commitment to Christ as the Lord of the church. So it asks for at least two years in training once a person decides he wants to do so. This means attending the School of Christian Living and taking basic courses on the Bible, doctrine, ethics, stewardship, and Christian growth, with electives in subjects such as speech, creative expression, and prayer.

Those in the school have dinner together first, and take turns in preparing it. There is exciting discussion on all kinds of topics during this meal, and it is followed by a worship period; then the different classes meet from 8:00 till 9:30 P.M.

After having attended the school, the applicant has to make a written statement about his faith, spiritual self-discipline, use of money, and areas in which he knows he is weak and needs help. A sponsor is chosen from among the members to work and counsel with the applicant, supervise his required reading, and help him study and memorize the commitment he must make before the congregation. There are also certain "disciplines" to choose, not as rules for pious perfection, but as responses to life and the grace of God. He must also commit himself to some branch of service to the church.

Members are continually exploring and looking for different forms of service and mission, to each other and the world. They own a farm and work it themselves, as well as using it for retreats. They have a rehabilitation center for alcoholics and psychiatric cases.

Their coffee shop, "The Potter's House," has attracted great interest. At one time, the pastor, Gordon Cosby, and his wife attended a church in New England. Its chilly remoteness saddened them, and when they entered the coffee shop in the same town, they noticed warm, friendly atmosphere and conversation. Surely, this was the kind of atmosphere in which Christians should be living their faith! And why not? Was there any reason why a church should not meet in a restaurant, or even a tavern? And so the idea for the coffee shop was born, and emerged as "The Potter's House." Here, people from all walks of life—artists, politicians, housewives, beatniks, businessmen—come to drink coffee and talk; to see art exhibits; to hear plays read and music; and be served by members of the church who are ready to join the discussions or answer questions.

This church has aroused great interest all over the world, and not only interest, but envy. It took great courage to dare to do something so radically different and yet based on the New Testament. Nor is the church related to any denomination.

Perhaps, in the years to come there will be others who will

dare to cut the cords that tie down the conventional concept of a church just as Gulliver was tied down by the Lilliputians.

Suggestions for Discussion and Action:

How do the members of your group react to the idea of strict requirements in order to become a member of a church? Young people in the Church of the Saviour choose their own godparents from among the members for guidance and help. They also attend the School of Christian Living. Any comment on this?

Many churches and youth groups all over the world have come to realize that we tend to take church membership as lightly as joining a club. Many have drawn up their own disciplines, within the usual church framework.

Instead of the usual additional resources at the end of this chapter, you will find some of these disciplines, and you may want to study them. You might even want to compile one of your own for a limited time, to see if you feel the need for one too.

Self-discipline is not an isolated thing—nor should it be!—but is achieved in cooperation with others sharing it too. See the next chapter for more about this.

Chapter IX gives accounts of other coffee house ventures.

Prayer:

"Now to him who by the power at work within us is able to do far more abundantly than all that we ask or think, to him be glory in the church and in Christ Jesus to all generations, for ever and ever. Amen." (Eph. 3:20-21.)

SOME NEW DISCIPLINES WITHIN THE CHURCH

The present minimum discipline of the Church of the Saviour:

"We covenant with Christ and one another to:

Meet God daily in a set time of prayer

Let God confront us daily through the Scriptures

Grow in love for the brotherhood and all people, remembering the command, 'Love one another as I have loved you'

Worship weekly—normally with our church
Be a vital contributing member of one of the groups
Give proportionately, beginning at a tithe of our incomes
Confess and ask the help of our fellowship should we fail in
these expressions of devotion." [12]

The Yoke of Christ:

This began in 1960 with a small group of Episcopalian teenagers
in Rhode Island and has spread to other states. Members wear a
gold yoke-shaped pin, the emblem of the Yokefellow movement
started several years ago by D. Elton Trueblood, who gave the teenagers permission to use the emblem.

The Rule of the Yoke of Christ:

1: To worship God every Sunday without fail. . . .

2: To receive holy communion at least once a month, and
always on Christmas, Easter and Whitsunday.

3: To make a thorough examination of myself at least four
times a year, and whenever my conscience is burdened
with grievous sin, to consult a priest for counsel, and, if
necessary, for absolution.

4: To choose a form of self-denial which will aid me in
establishing control of my appetites and . . . to adhere
faithfully to my choice.

5: To read the Bible daily according to some definite plan,
and to pray daily for the rule of Christ in the hearts of
men.

6: To endeavor always to conduct my social life . . . to meet
God's approval; and never to make or sign any agreement
which makes impossible the fulfillment of my obligations
to my marriage partner, our children and my church.

7: To give sacrificially to my church, using the Biblical tithe
as a norm.

8: To serve my church willingly and actively in some manner
agreed upon between me and my rector . . .

9: To report once each three months to the diocesan youth
advisor . . . as to my fidelity in carrying out this rule.

Dunfermline Abbey Bible Class:

This commitment was drawn up by a group of Scottish teen-agers.

"*We Believe* that Christ is the Lord of all: whatever intellectual problems this may create in other spheres, we believe that this Lordship must start from our own situation. We believe that we are called to do His work among our neighbors: that this must be done, not with an eye to our own status, but by humble open-ness to the needs of others. We believe that the Christian life is marked by charity, compassion, and simple good fun. We believe that people matter.

We Admit that this attempt at serious discipleship has not been a complete success: in part this has been due to our being too sensitive of our own feelings and too insensitive to the feelings of others; in part also to the fact that we have not made sufficient effort in the face of odds against us. This discipleship obviously means a total change of outlook for us all.

We, therefore, *intend* to follow Christ regardless of where He may lead us (recognizing that He may lead us to a Cross), and with no thought to material consequences. We do not know what may come of this experience, but we pledge that we shall not let it go for nothing." [13]

East Harlem Protestant Parish:

This is a pattern of discipline not only for the clergy, but for all Christians, "to be applied at only a few points with special reference to the individual Christian's own calling within the life of the church." [14]

1: *The Ordered Day:* Beginning the day with thankfulness, and a plan to seek to use it as we feel God would wish it; with prayer, Bible reading, and Bible study. Ending the day with intercession and petition, and commiting our lives into God's hands.

2: *Holy Communion:* Attending on the first Sunday of each month.

3: *Participation in an "enabling group"*: Bible study in small prayer fellowships, or cell groups, constantly checking to make sure there is relationship to the real problems of life as Christians in the world, and not merely pious introversion.

4: *Discussing our Christian faith monthly with another*: Discussion with a brother, in a straightforward manner, as to whether or not we are really adhering to the discipline.

5: *Give a definite share of our income to God's Church*: "In recognition of our dependence upon God, we render unto him, in joyful thanksgiving, a part of what he has given us." [15]

6: *To participate in at least one community organization working for justice or brotherhood*: Reminding us of our responsibility to witness in concrete ways to the love of God in Christ.

7: *To exercise the particular ministry which has been given us*: Seeking to find, in the light of Eph. 4:11-12, our own particular gift to contribute to the fellowship of the church.

Yeovil Industrial Order:

The detail of this order was worked out by men working in industry in the town of Yeovil, in England. They decided on commitment to a life of prayer, worship, Bible study, service, and discipline. They chose, as the prayer of their order, the one beginning, "Lord, make me an instrument of your peace," [16] and they pray it every day at 11 A.M. as they think of each other.

Iona Associates:

This is the vow taken by men, women, and youth on June 9 and November 11: "By the grace of God and in company with other seekers, I dedicate myself anew to a closer discipline in response to this free gift to me of life."

chapter VII

CHRISTIANITY = COMMUNITY

1. MAN IS ALONE—YET NO MAN IS ALONE

Scripture: Rom. 14:7-12 ("None of us lives to himself.")

Reading:

Do we agree with the words of John Donne, "No man is an island"? Man has to balance two halves of his being, just as he balances and reconciles love and hate; hot and cold; dislike for Bach and liking for folk music; prejudice against Presbyterians and love for Lutherans; disdain for croquet and a yen for surfing.

Yet in this "shook up generation," as it has been called, there has been a drift to extremes, from the solitary nonconformist and his pad, to the chameleon-like conformity of the crowd or gang. The church gets put to one side as being unable to speak to either situation with relevance, but it is only in the Christian community that these two extremes, this chalk and this cheese, can live together in harmony.

Christians have been known through the ages for a special kind of love for one another, a fellowship called "koinonia." This is something that takes place naturally when those of the same congregation, or social group meet together, but it is much more difficult for it to take place between those who, quite frankly, regard each other with dislike. Yet we know that Christ told his disciples to go out and minister "to all nations," not just to their friends and relatives.

What does all this have to do with the need for man to know he is alone, yet never alone? It means that as a Christian he must face himself as Christ sees him and take his place in the Christian community with others who have also faced themselves as Christ sees them and who accept one another.

"It is a call to love and save not the nice, but the nasty; not the lovable but the unlovely, the hard, the narrow, and the embittered, and the tiresome, who are so much worse. To love irrespective of merit or opinion or personal preference; to love even those who offend our taste." [1]

Suggestions for Discussion and Action:

Read the suggested scripture again. Have you ever thought about the relationship between the words "community," "communication," "communion," and "Holy Communion"?

What is meant by the words "communion of the saints" in the Apostles' Creed? Did you know that you were a saint? (If not, look up the meaning of the word!)

Why is it that when the World Council of Churches meets, its members are still unable to take Communion together? You might aid your understanding of this by inviting members from another church denomination to meet with you, for a Christian dialogue on the subject and an explanation of their understanding of Holy Communion. Before doing this you will need to be sure you understand your own form of it. Here it is again! You must know yourself before you know others, and you cannot know others till you know yourself.

Until recently there was a gulf of suspicion between Protestants and Roman Catholics. Ireland was one of the places where this gulf was at its widest and most hostile. In Protestant Northern Ireland no one believed there could be such a thing as a "good" Roman Catholic; a "better-dead-than-Catholic" kind of outlook prevailed. Recently a Protestant youth group invited an outsider to give his viewpoint of this situation and then asked a Roman Catholic priest to give the feelings of the other side. Later, a lawyer helped with a study of the political implications of this religious feud. New understanding is emerging, of course.

Can you do something like this in your area, with some group from whom you feel separated?

See Chapter IX for accounts of German youth and reconciliation, the Anti-Defamation League, and Agape.

Prayer:

One of the characteristics of Christian community is the ability to forgive and be forgiven. You may want to use this ancient prayer and its response. In a monastery the abbot would ask forgiveness of the brothers, and after they forgave him, they confessed their sins and were absolved.

V. "I confess to God Almighty, and in the sight of the whole company of heaven, that I have sinned exceedingly in thought, word, and deed through my fault, my own fault, my own most grievous fault, wherefore, I pray God Almighty to have mercy upon me.

R. *"May the Almighty and Merciful Lord grant you pardon, absolution, and remission of all your sins, time for amendment of life, and the comfort of His Holy Spirit."*

V. "Amen." [2]

(The above to be repeated: the Responder taking the Versicle)

2. THE CONFUSIONS OF MARY AND MARTHA

Scripture: Luke 10:38-42 ("You are anxious and troubled about many things.")

Reader:

"There have been many Marys and Marthas since the days of Jesus. Some serene and confident with their way of living; some with feelings of guilt; some pointing the finger at one another; and some with a split personality, as they attempt to justify their actions according to the demands of our split-level culture.

"*First Mary:* Yesterday, when walking in the park, I saw an old couple sitting on a bench, bone-weary, ivory-old; and the tree behind them leaf-weary, stark-cold, etched as they were. And I turned to the young man beside me and said, 'I cannot go with you. I must paint this. Now.' And I did, but I have not seen the young man again.

"*First Martha:* Today I gloat in secret, holding it in, and yet so proud of my rug-washing, weed-pulling, floor-waxing day! My good work is publicized by the fragrant smell of apple pie coming from the oven (two for dinner, and eight for the freezer, of course!). I also cleaned behind the refrigerator, and no one knows that but me. I am a housewife, and glory in doing my work well, in this aluminum-screened, air-conditioned, air-freshened, ready-for-inspection-any-minute home of mine. I am sure that John my husband will be glad with me . . . Oh, no, John *no!* Not on my clean floor!

"*Second Mary:* If I marry Jim I will have to give up my career, for he thinks that a woman's place is in the home. I know I can make a home for him, but I want to do other things too. My fingers are trained, my mind is trained, and my heart leads me to the surgical, neurological, pathological, gynaecological patient who needs me, in the hospital where nurses are so few. I would much rather boil instruments than potatoes. And yet, I love Jim!

"*Second Martha:* Susan has such odd ideas. Here we were at Tom's party, everyone having a ball; everyone laughing, everyone talking, everyone dancing, way out beyond themselves in happiness. Suddenly Susan says 'I'm sorry, I must go. I have to study for an English test tomorrow.' And she went. You can imagine what that did to the party. We all began thinking about that English test too. Susan just has no sense of proportion!

"*Third Mary:* I hate Mrs. Jones! She asked me why I had not time to help serve at the church dinner, if I had time to go to two hours of choir practice that night. She said she had to give up the luxury of singing for more important things!

"*Third Martha:* How I envy Mary! She can understand Karl Barth and read as fast as President Kennedy. I can only pronounce ex-is-ten-tial-ism when I am by myself, and can say it slowly. I wish I knew what it meant, but then, I'm only a Martha, so what's the point in trying?

"*All the Marys:* We are confused. Something is missing!

"*All the Marthas:* We are confused too. What can we do?

"*Marys:* We think some things are so much more important than the mere mechanics of living.

"*Marthas:* We pride ourselves on doing the mechanics of living well, and yet we want to do other things too.

"*Reader:* You are too busy. You have never taken the time to sit quietly in the sun, for no reason at all. You have never discovered that we need to turn over everything we think we can do, and want to do, to God. Only those who have done this, who put their whole lives in his keeping; who know how to drop the clutter of decision and conflict, guilt and envy; who know that he gave each of us certain gifts to explore and develop, only these can turn to him and find out how to become inwardly whole. Nothing can be achieved unless we withdraw from the world now and then, here and there, in little snatches of solitude to renew our strength. Then we can go back to our life with others—less a Martha, more a Mary; more a Martha, less a Mary." [3]

Suggestions for Discussion and Action:

Read the scripture again. What did Jesus mean by his answer to Martha? He said "one thing is needful," explaining to her that elaborate preparations were not necessary for his reception.

The reading you have just heard gives examples of the Mary-Martha conflict in society today. Open a discussion of these conflicts by asking, "What is the role of a woman today?" "How much are women confused by 'the clutter of decision and conflict, guilt and envy?'"

Supposing Jesus had come to Martha's house when she was not home, and her sister Mary received him. If she had not given him the traditional water to wash his feet, and food and drink, but had wanted to listen to his teachings at once, would Jesus have rebuked her instead? In other words, there are basic practical things that women must do—such as cooking, cleaning, and child care—but there are times when they should be kept to a minimum.

The reading suggests that we all need to retreat from the world now and then, to see our lives in better perspective. You might want to plan a retreat to discuss these things and help each person become aware of his or her particular gifts and the gifts of others. Then plan ways in which each one in your group will have the opportunity to use these gifts.

You might want to work this out on a Michael-Mark basis of conflict too! (The man who can tune a motor versus the man who can tune a violin!)

Prayer:

Lord God, we come before you with our fragmented and hurried lives. Heal us with the knowledge of your peace which passes all understanding. Send us back into your world no longer fretting over things we feel we should do and know we cannot do, but confident of your gift ready to unfold, to each one of us. May we prove to be worthy of your son, Jesus Christ, in whose name we pray. Amen.

3. MEMBERS OF THE HOUSEHOLD OF GOD

Scripture: Eph. 2:19-22 ("Members of the household of God.")

Reading:

We live in an era of experts, of highly skilled technicians, and professional men, and the knowledge accumulated and applied in each particular field has become so complicated that the ordinary layman leaves everything to these experts.

Occasionally, you will hear someone say, "Of course, I'm only a layman, but I think. . . ." and the expert will look at him as if he is thinking, "Fools rush in where angels fear to tread." Or, the layman who speaks up may remind us of Job who questioned God's actions, and then laid his hand over his mouth when he found he had uttered what he did not understand.

Who is this groveling little layman, who sometimes had the temerity to speak out of turn? The word "laity" comes from the Greek, meaning "the people," and a Christian layman is, quite simply, not one of the clergy.

"The assumption is that a layman is one of the privates in God's army; and the officers are the clergy. As if there were two grades of Christians—first class: parsons, and second class: laity. The first class have the job of running the church, of deciding the doctrine and administering the Sacraments and preaching the sermons and, above all, setting a good example. They have to be first-class in moral standards. The second-class Christians, the laity, don't have quite the same status in the church (or probably in heaven hereafter.)" [4]

In recent years there has been a surge of interest in the place of the layman, not with the idea of a quiet revolution to overthrow the clergy, but to remind the layman that he and the clergy together make up the church and all are equal in the sight of God, though all have different tasks.

The church, whose foundation is Jesus Christ our Lord, is much more than the events within a certain typical building, and the church can be the church whether a member of the clergy is present or not. We need to remember that Jesus said, "Where two or three are gathered in my name, there am I in the midst of them." So the church is assembled when people meet to pray together in a home, or attend a juvenile court to learn more about delinquency, or meet during the noon hour in a factory to study ethical behavior, or paint the house of an elderly woman who lives alone, or talk about every subject under the sun in a coffee house organized by the church. In all these things no clergy need be present, for here the layman is being the church. Yet behind all this lay action the clergy are still needed to lead and teach, to point the way, and to fulfill their appointed tasks—the administration of the Sacraments and the preaching of the Word.

The layman has been looking at the world through bifocal lenses —one is his everyday life, one is his churchly life. Now he needs to see that these two must become one, for God is in them both and the church must become world centered.

Suggestions for Discussion and Action:

Read the selected scripture again, and then try to read Romans 12 as translated by J. B. Phillips. Use this as the basis for your discussion of the role of the layman today.

What part does the layman play in your church, *out in the world?* Are you included in this, or do those of you who are under twenty-one feel like third-class Christians?

If you feel a third-class Christian, is this the way older members make you feel, or is it because you are only making a third-class effort to be a Christian layman? What could you do in your own group, or with others of all ages, *out in the world?*

Prayer:

Lord, we stand ready. Our ears and our eyes are open. Our hands wait for their work. Use us, we pray, use even us to serve mankind, out in thy world today. Amen.

4. 400,000 SANG TOGETHER AT THE KIRCHENTAG

Scripture: Rom. 10:14-18 ("Their voice has gone out to all the earth.")

Reading:

A sixteen-year-old boy stayed with a German family during the summer of 1963, and this is what he wrote home:

"Have you ever heard of Doctor Reinhold von Thadden? Probably not. It was through his idea that the world-renowned German Kirchentag (Church Congress) came into being.

"On the 28th of July 400,000 participants from all over West Germany, and other parts of Europe and the world, assembled at the industrial city of Dortmund for the Eleventh Kirchentag.

"In order to arrive in time for the Morning Service we had to get up at 5 a.m., for the train left at 6 o'clock. Immediately we stepped on board we noticed an atmosphere which was completely different from a normal train journey. Everyone was very friendly and happy, and soon they began to sing together as only the German people can. We reached Dortmund about 9:30, and we had to hurry to reach the church before 10 o'clock. In spite of our haste, I noticed the crowded streets, the banners with purple crosses, and huge red placards showing a crown of thorns. At five to 10 we arrived at the church and slowly marched in. All the seats were soon filled and as the ministers processed to the aisle, to the accompaniment of a great fanfare of trumpets, towards the simple wooden cross, one really felt the triumph of Christ. The Communion Service came at the end. Each row of people walked up to the altar, and each worshipper received a wafer imprinted with the symbol of the Kirchentag, and each drank from the Common Cup. As one stood there in front of the altar, while the congregation sang and the organ played, there was a great feeling of being in a great family.

"After the service we had dinner, and then proceeded to the final meeting of the Kirchentag. All 400,000 people were assembled together in a vast sports stadium. Towering high above everything else were three gigantic wooden crosses. The service began with a hymn. I shall never forget the sound of four hundred thousand voices blending perfectly with two thousand brass instruments. As the meeting progressed there were talks by von Thadden and other Church leaders, prayers for East Germany, Church Unity, and for those disabled in the war, and finally the Lord's Prayer. The meeting ended in an unforgettable blaze of glory as the hymn "Now thank we all our God" was sung by that great multitude of people, joined by the brass instruments and four huge bells. It was a truly magnificent experience, and a fitting end to a wonderful day." [5]

Suggestions for Discussion and Action:

Read the scripture again, noticing the line "faith comes from what is heard." Do you think that faith would be more likely to come to those who took part in a tremendous gathering like the Kirchentag? Could you imagine something like this in our country?

After discussion go on to explain that there is much more to the Kirchentag than the one day attended by this boy. It is a five-day gathering with over 450 events.

Dortmund is in the heart of the great Ruhr industrial area, and many of its men are coal miners or steel workers. This is the kind of place where no one takes much notice of the church, and life is hard and dangerous. So, the theme for that year was "To Live with Conflicts." The boy mentioned red placards showing a crown of thorns. This crown was made of barbed wire, relating the suffering of man today with the suffering of Christ.

Each day began with worship in all the Dortmund churches. Then people gathered in nearby centers for Bible study and discussion. Many sessions were in the afternoon or evening so that those in heavy industry could come after work. In addition to the main program, there were musical events, ranging from Bach cantatas to Negro spirituals and new types of religious songs; photography and book exhibits; workshops in new forms of worship, fellowship, and artistic expression.

Young people's groups used chamber-music-style jazz with the words of new modern hymns. One group gave an explanation of

Jesus' call to discipleship. This was followed by a panel of young people who raised objections and made comments.

How is the Kirchentag different from the mass rallies of Billy Graham?

On the last day, Dr. von Thadden said, "He who by faith can live with conflicts is truly free. The theme of his life will no longer be escape, but remaining in the place where God has put him." [6] What does this say to your group?

Prayer:

Lord, expose us to situations where our faith is challenged and given a chance to grow. Give us the grace to be good listeners. Give us the courage to face the problems of life, as Christ would have us face them. Amen.

5. A BRIDGE BETWEEN THE CHURCH AND THE WORLD

Scripture: Dan. 5:1-8, 17-27 ("You have been weighed in the balances and found wanting.")

Reading:

Whenever there is discussion of the renewal of the church, there is usually mention of what is happening in Germany today. Perhaps it will be about the great gatherings for the Kirchentag or the Evangelical Academies, and often there is talk of a town with the odd name of Bad Boll. Does this mean that the church is stronger in Germany, and that we can learn from it? No and yes! In other words, the church is weaker there, but we can learn from what is happening as it may happen to us too!

The church in Germany has been "weighed in the balances and found wanting." When the Nazi party tried to stamp out the Christian faith, it very nearly succeeded. The faith of the majority of the people had so little meaning that it provided neither root nor anchor when the time of testing came, and when air raids devastated the country. Too many were Christians in name only. Now they are not even that, for only a remnant call themselves Christians; but it is a dynamic, living remnant searching for ways to speak to those who have turned away from God.

In the United States today, about 60 percent call themselves Christians. We think of ourselves as a "nation under God," and are a little smug about it. But Thomas Oden has written of the Organization Man who said out loud, "I believe in God the Father Almighty, Maker of heaven and earth," while in his heart he said, "Nobody believes that any more." [7] If the same chain of events that struck Germany struck us today, or if nuclear war came, how well would that 60 percent hold up under the strain?

What is happening in Germany? What is an "academy"? An academy is not a college, but a conference center where people meet together to discuss some subject. You may think it sounds like what we would call a "retreat," and in a way it is, for often some beautiful place is chosen. Yet a retreat is a withdrawal to strengthen the inner life of an already committed Christian, whereas the academy tries to reach people on the edge of the church or quite outside it. It is the church trying to create a bridge to the world, trying to begin a conversation again, willing to listen and willing to answer questions. It is the church uniting with the world to grapple with problems of man today.

The first Evangelical Academy met at Bad Boll in Southern Germany, in 1945. Now there are eighteen of them, in different parts of the country, serving the people and the problems peculiar to each area. The first conference, for workers, turned out to be between Christians themselves, as the invitations were sent through the local parish. Now, invitations and announcements go straight to the Trades Unions and management, so that those who come are even hostile to the church, or apathetic, as well as those who are committed Christians.

For example, eighty representatives from the Daimler-Betz car factory in Stuttgart came to one conference at Bad Boll, to discuss industrial and human relations problems within their own factory. All levels of the personnel were represented. The firm paid the conference expenses and made up the loss of wages, but no one felt it was organized by the management as the unions were there too.

There is no attempt to convert anyone, nor to defend the Christian viewpoint, but there is a period of Bible study relevant to the theme of the conference, and there is worship every morning and evening.

What are the results of all this? Is the church becoming stronger in Germany? Each year sixty thousand men and women take part in the academy programs, yet there is little change in the parish life. People go home from a conference with new ideas and new understanding, and find their church just as it was, steeped in out-of-datè tradition. The academies cannot survive unless the institutional church is drawn into the regeneration that must come. If the church is not regenerated, it may disappear altogether.

There are now twenty-six lay academies in the United States and Canada. Their problem is to explore what they should be, for this is not Germany, and our problems are different. For example, the Evangelical Academies get substantial financial support from the government. A suggestion that we do this in our country could start another civil war!

There is great demand for further religious instruction for the awakening layman, who knows he must have better understanding of his beliefs, before he ventures out into the world for Christian dialogue and action.

Suggestions for Discussion and Action:

Discuss the suggested scripture. What did the handwriting on the wall say to Belshazzar, to the Germans, and what might it say to us?

Is there weakness in our own group, in our own church? Do we need to stir up a discussion of the subject? As Christians, are we lacking in a knowledge of the Bible; its application to our faith; and its relevance to the problems of life outside the church building.

It is obvious that weakness in individuals leads to a weak church and a weak denomination. The responsibility lies right where we are. What can we do about it?

Is there any reason why young people should not join with adults in a study program? This has been done on retreats, but why should it not take place in the local church too, or the community? Who should be invited, and how? You might try the Evangelical Academy method, and invite those not on the church mailing list, but all those in your church or college; young married couples; young single adults working in the community; maybe those working part time while at school or college—the list could go on and on. If you cannot get addresses, use posters and announcements in the local press and over radio or TV. Choose a topic of vital interest to the groups invited. What are the dangers in lay academies or study programs? (Can they develop too much emphasis on intellectual discussion, and not enough on action? Can they bypass the local church?)

See Chapter IX for details of some of the lay academies and retreat centers in the United States.

Prayer:

"Let us recall with penitence the small part the Church in the West has taken in the social and industrial changes of the last two hundred years, and the weak impact which the Church makes upon the industrial world today. . . .

"Let us pray for a spirit of service to the community in all involved in ownership, management and labour; for a deeper valuation of human relationships in industry; . . . for God's blessing on experiments in partnership, profit-sharing, and planning to meet difficulties; for God's blessing on pastoral and evangelistic experiments, especially on industrial chaplains, and priest-workmen.

"May Christ be acknowledged as the Lord of all life!" Amen.[8]

6. THE IONA COMMUNITY

Scripture: Jer. 6:10-14 ("They have healed the wound of my people lightly, saying, 'Peace, peace,' when there is no peace.")

Reading:

Iona is a small island off the coast of Scotland. In the winter it is blown with spume and spray; but when summer comes, there are flowers all through the short grass, and men and women come to visit the Abbey, to walk on the white sand, and look across the blue green water, for Iona is a beautiful place.

Over fourteen hundred years ago, Columba and his monks came over the sea from Ireland. They settled there and carried the light of Christianity to many countries at a time when the Roman Empire was beginning to crumble under the inroads of the barbarians. Many years later the Benedictine order built an abbey there, but in time it was deserted too. Still the feeling persisted that Iona was a holy place, for had not Columba prophesied that it would always be so?

In 1938 the Iona Community was founded when George Mac-Leod decided to rebuild the Abbey. He came with a handful of young men, disturbed by the gulf between the unemployed men in the Depression and the church. He felt sure that there must be a renewal of the link between work and worship, and that men must do both together if the church was to have meaning in their lives. As the years went by, more men came to join them—some ministers, some craftsmen, and a common discipline was followed.

Those who come as guests to Iona are expected to work also, to attend the early morning service, and share in the celebration of Holy Communion. They never forget that service, and the fresh loaves of homemade bread that are carried in from the kitchen and then taken to the tables in the refectory for dinner.

"What makes the impact is essentially not the craft of the ministers but the ministry of the craftsmen. It is the fact that it is their worship. The reason for the morning service is that men are going to work and for the evening service that men have finished work: the fact that men are there in their working clothes, not a gesture but because these are their daily clothes—it is this fact that makes worship suddenly relevant. Those who attend, campers, Conference-attenders, holiday makers, don't feel that this is a service put on for their benefit or their instruction. They know that it is a service that goes on when they are not there and which goes on, led by a joiner or a mason, when no minister is there. It is part of a life into which they have been drawn for a time: a life in which work and worship are naturally joined together, where men are working on a real job of building and where corporate worship is a celebration of their work." [9]

You may be wondering what connection there is between the life on this faraway island and unemployed men on a city street. Plenty! The work and worship on Iona, the conferences and discussions, are times of renewal and planning that take place during the summer months. For the rest of the year, members are scattered in industry throughout Scotland, or in different parts of the world, including the United States. Their hub is then the Community House in Glasgow, where young people, Sunday school teachers, alcoholics anonymous, Scottish dancers, study groups, and a host of other groups meet and talk and eat.

In the thick of it, when he is not traveling all over the world talking about the Iona Community, is its leader, George F. MacLeod. This is what he has said about the task of the church today:

"I am not a 'perfectionist'—I am not arguing in effect that 'if only Christians would become involved then we could expect the dawning of a new world of plenty, brotherhood and peace!' But I would share the strong conviction that if Christians do not more liberally add their salt to the boiling mixture that is the present turmoil then, bereft of seasoning, it will boil over to the scalding, it may be, of the whole world. This involvement is the King's business and it requireth haste." [10]

George MacLeod knows—as the prophet Jeremiah did—that we cannot pretend all is well and say, "Peace, peace, when there is no peace."

Suggestions for Discussion and Action:

One example of the Iona Community's involvement with the everyday world was shown at the time of the 1,400 centenary celebrations in June 1963. People came from all over the world to remember the day when Columba landed on Iona and to look forward with the Community as they celebrated their twenty-fifth anniversary. There was a procession, great men spoke, and TV equipment braved the trip to the island to bring the events to many countries in Europe. One day a small boat arrived, as a gift from the Presbyterian Church of Ireland. It had come across the same wild stretch of water navigated by Columba in the sixth century, and was blessed by the church dignitaries when it landed in the same bay. This was no elaborate gift to be set aside as a reminder of the celebrations. It was an ordinary, stubby little row boat which had been used for years off the Irish coast, catching herring, mackerel, and lobster. Complete with a motor, it was put to practical use by the Community, and has hauled gravel, been used by the youth camps, and used for general transportation to and from the island.

Notice that there was a service for the blessing of the boat before it was put to work. In Columba's day, there were prayers for the blessing of all forms of work, including the animals or things that helped man with his labors. Have we lost sight of this today? What connection is there between your *work*—and worship? (There are vague prayers about man and his toil, but rarely are they specific.) Does a Christian doctor ask that his new X-ray equipment be blessed? Is there a prayer at the installation of new lighting on a dark street? (Probably not, because of the entanglements of church and State!)

What can you do, so that there is more connection between work and worship in your group? Are you adding any salt?

See Chapter IX for more information about the Iona Community, its discipline, its youth associates. And read about Kirkridge (page 218), a retreat center in Maine having close ties with Iona. There is also mention of the Iona influence on pages 47-49.

A Prayer of the Iona Community:

"Spirit of the living Christ, come upon us in the glory of thy risen power;

"Spirit of the living Christ, come upon us all in the humility of thy wondrous love;

"Spirit of the living Christ, come upon us that new life may course within our veins, new love bind us together in one family, a new vision of the Kingdom of Love spur us on to serve thee with a fearless passion. For thy sake we ask it. Amen." [11]

7. TAIZÉ—AND UNDERSTANDING BETWEEN ALL CHRISTIANS

Scripture: John 13:34, 35 ("Have love for one another.")

Reading:

At seven in the morning, at noon, and in the evening, the brothers of the Taizé Community in France put on their white robes and file into church. The services there consist of the singing of psalms, Scripture lessons, and prayers. When the Scriptures are read, the Bible is carried out into the congregation. Prominent in the prayers is intercession for the unity of the church from its fragmented divisions.

For the rest of the day, the brothers put on ordinary work clothes. One, a medical doctor, serves as physician for the area, others are agriculturalists and have organized a milk cooperative for the farmers, as well as milking the Community's prize herd of cows. Some are clerks, and the arts are represented in pottery sculpture, painting, architecture, and fine printing. Most of the men are laymen from a variety of Protestant faiths, but there are some who are ministers too.

From the original seven who organized the Community in 1947 the numbers have grown, and in 1964 there were sixty brothers. At first they worshiped in the little Roman Catholic church in the village—which was startling enough in itself—but now there is also the new Church of the Reconciliation, built on a hill by German work teams as a symbol of repentance to France. This church is Protestant, and beneath it is a Roman Catholic chapel, and beside it a new Orthodox center where it is hoped that monks from Russia and Greece will be able to live together. Huge crowds come to worship at Taizé—tourists, students, theologians, and those from groups as different as the Pentecostals or the Salvation Army. All seem to understand each other in the warmth and vigor of the simple service.

We hear so much of the divisions that divide the churches, and we usually blame it on theological or institutional differences. Roger Schutz, the founder and Prior, believes that many of the divisions are due to prejudices we learn in childhood or in social or ethic backgrounds. Mention a "red-hot Gospel" message to an Episcopalian or a Presbyterian, and a wall of suspicion shoots up at once. Let a pastor suggest using candles in one kind of church, and there is a cry of "Romanism, Popery!" Yet, often these groups, with their totally different concepts of what it means to be a part of Christ's church, know very little about each other's practices at all. No wonder those outside the church ridicule her divisions!

The brothers of Taizé believe that when Christ gave the second great commandment, he meant that we should love our neighbors in the other kinds of churches, as well as our neighbors out in the world.

All the brothers have taken the perpetual vows of "community of goods, celibacy, and acceptance of authority." Only about half of them live at Taizé, although they all return to meet together for one week each year. Each has his own trade or profession. For example, one drives a fork-lift truck for the General Electric Company in England, one is at the Chapel of Unity in Coventry Cathedral, one group is in South America teaching the cooperative agricultural methods they have used at Taizé. Some travel widely speaking on the ecumenical movement; the Prior was invited as a special observer of the Vatican Council; and three brothers have been in Randolph, New Jersey, forming the nucleus of an American community.

Wherever they go, they are committed to make sure that the primary reason for their work is the improvement of Christian unity.

Suggestions for Discussion and Action:

After the selected scripture is read at Taizé, there is silence for a few minutes of meditation upon what has been read. Why don't you read the selected scripture again and call for five minutes of silence to think about the words you have just heard.

What are the things that prevent us from loving people who are different from us? Do you agree with Prior Schutz, that we are tangled up with the prejudices absorbed in childhood?

Try asking for instant (and honest!) reactions to certain words, such as "Jew," "saved," "Blood of the Lamb," "Jehovah's Witness," "speaking in tongues," "evangelist," "genuflection," "confession," "rosary," "faith healing." Find out how much the meanings of these words are really understood or have been distorted by prejudice and ignorance.

Try inviting a group from another denomination, or sect, totally different from yours. You might have a meal together, and some recreation, then suggest some service project for the community as a whole, in which you could work together. (Some may look on you as "lost sheep" and refuse to come or be forbidden to do so, but keep trying!)

Prayer:

Lord God, we are ashamed of the divisions that divide us and the prejudices that cloud our understanding of each other. Make us eager to learn and listen, and make us quick to admit our misconceptions. Unite us in the simple task of following Christ, in whose name we pray together. Amen.

181

ADDITIONAL WORSHIP RESOURCES

Scripture:

I Thess. 4:9-12 ("You yourselves have been taught by God to love one another.")

Rom. 15:1-6 ("Live in . . . harmony with one another.")

Luke 9:46-48 ("Whoever receives me receives him who sent me.")

Phil. 1:3-18; 2:1-11 ("You are all partakers with me of grace.")

Eph. 4:1-7, 11-16, 25-32 ("Forbearing one another in love.")

Jas. 3 ("Righteousness is sown in peace by those who make peace.")

John 15:12-17 ("Love one another as I have loved you.")

Matt. 5:21-24; 7:1-5 ("First be reconciled to your brother.")

Prayers:

"Let Thy power, O Christ, be in us all, to share the world's sufferings and redress its wrongs. Amen." [12]

"O Thou who hast created us with the ability to perceive and take attitudes toward our being and doing. . . .

"Enable us by . . . [thy] grace meaningfully to explore the nature of our human predicament in relation to ourselves, that we might more compassionately know, serve and understand the world in its despair, even as Thou hast known, served and understood us. Amen." [13]

Lord God, we thank you for our homes, our families, and our different abilities to work in many ways. Let us never forget those whose families live in discomfort, who long to work, yet cannot find employment. Help us, we earnestly pray, to join with others in striving to provide work for all men, so that the day may come when, together, we worship you through the joy of work. Amen.

Hymns:

In Christ There Is No East or West
God of the Nations, Hear Our Call
Christ for the World We Sing
Where Cross the Crowded Ways of Life
Rise Up, O Men of God
O Brother Man, Fold to Thy Heart Thy Brother
Be Thou My Vision
These Things Shall Be, a Loftier Race (to tune Truro)
O Where Are Kings and Empires Now?

chapter VIII

GLORY TO GOD IN THE HIGHEST

1. WHAT IS THIS THING CALLED GLORY?

Scripture: Luke 2:8-14 ("Glory to God in the highest.")

Reading:

"Glory to God in the highest." The words bring a reminder of Christmas—the first Christmas, and hosts of angels over a Bethlehem hillside; Christmases we have known ourselves, singing carols and hearing that passage from Luke, "the glory of the Lord shone around them, and they were filled with fear."

What is this shining word "glory"?

It runs like a light through both the Old and New Testaments. The glory of God shone in a burning bush. His glory was lodged in the Ark which the people carried with them on their wanderings. It was in the Holy of Holies of the great temple built by Solomon, under God's instruction, a place so holy that only the high priest might enter it, once a year.

But God's glory was not confined to a sanctuary. His work was glorious, and the psalmists described how he "stretched out the heavens like a tent," made "springs gush forth in the valleys," and caused "the grass to grow for the cattle" (Ps. 104:2, 10, 14). How he made the moon and the darkness and the sea "great and wide" (Ps. 104:25). God's mighty deeds inspired an awe in men, for his glory was as mysterious as it was wonderful, as frightening as a great storm, as amazing as a "still small voice" (I Kings 9:12). It made men aware that God was everlasting, and that they themselves would fade like flowers and wither away.

Then the radiant glory of God became man in Jesus Christ, and John wrote, "we have beheld his glory, glory as of the only Son from the Father" (John 1:14). With the death and resurrection of Christ, man was given the promise of becoming a part of the glory himself—his sins forgiven and death overcome. The book of Revelation looks to the glory beyond, and says, "All the angels stood round the throne . . . and worshiped God, saying, 'Amen! Blessing and glory and wisdom and thanksgiving and honor and power and might be to our God for ever and ever! Amen'" (Rev. 7:11-12).

It is no wonder that, the more miserable men are, the more they concentrate on this hope of glory after death and try to forget the hunger and cold, the rats, the persecution. No wonder that the sect type of church which dwells more on this subject, has more appeal to the miserable than does the WASP church (White Anglo-Saxon Protestant).

No wonder, either, that those who are quite comfortable do not spend much time thinking about the "hope of glory," and if they ever wonder about the locality or premises of heaven, they are apt to evaluate it coldly, like men preparing to sell one home and buy another. Such men are not even aware of the meaning of God's glory, either here on earth, or in the "highest."

Suggestions for Discussion and Action:

Instead of reading the suggested, familiar scripture again, read Rev. 7:9-17. Can you try to understand what this must say to those who are miserable in the world today? Discuss it, and then discuss what "glory to God in the highest" means to those in your group. How does man express this in his life?

Then read II Cor. 4:6 Halford E. Luccock has commented on this passage. "God appears as a face; He looks on us, and on the whole human family, through the eyes of Jesus Christ. What eyes they were, lighted with sympathy, forgiveness, and yet demanding eyes.

"We meet the glory of God in 'that one face.' . . .

"One of the primary tasks of life is to keep the wonder of the glory of God in the face of Christ. One of the risks of any life is to have that wonder fade into the light of common day. We tend to take the glory for granted. When awe and wonder are allowed to slip out of our lives, the glory is lost in the gray of plodding days. When we take the miracle of life for granted, a withering blight of the soul sets in." [1]

Prayer: A modern version of Psalm 8.

> *Lord God Almighty*
> how majestic is your name in all the earth
> in the stars and sun and moon
> in the world, and all living things.
> what is man
> and who are we
> that you should love us and care for us?
> and yet—
> you have loved us with an everlasting love
> you have made us and given us life
> you have sent your son to die for us.
> O *Lord, Our Lord*—
> *How majestic is your name in all the earth!*
> *We will praise you, now and always. Amen.*[2]

2. PRAISE GOD FROM WHOM ALL BLESSINGS FLOW

Scripture: Ps. 150:1-2, 6 ("Praise the Lord!")

Reading:

"Solo 1 (loud, strong):
  Praise God from Whom all blessings flow,
  In moving, surging life today.
"Solo 2 (quick and light):
  For sparkling water hurrying down,
  For fish that gleam within its depths,
"Solo 3 (medium); then (slower):
  For flowers that burst like flags in air
  And with their scent draw bumbling bees;

"Solo 1 (quicker):
  For birds that sweep and soar and dive,
  And make bright patterns in the sky;
"Solo 2 (medium):
    For smaller birds with rippling song
    Within the greenness of a tree;
"Solo 3 (quick then slow and quiet):
  For comic chipmunks on a log
  That's etched with fallen leaves, with moss,
  Pale fungi, twigs and seeds,
  With little things that drift and blow
  To settle, sleep, and wake again;
"Solo 1 (medium):
  From caterpillar into moth, and acorn into tree
"Solo 2 (quick):
  For insects organized, like ants
  To hurry round like busy men;
"Solo 3 (slow):
  Or those that plod with measured tread,
  Like beetles, or the rippling snail.
"Solo 1 (medium):
  Praise God for all his gifts to men,
"Solo 2 (medium):
  The grace to walk, to run, to swim,

"Solo 3 (slower):
  For ears to hear the sound of trees,
  The song of birds, the chipmunk's call;
"Solo 2 (slower):
  For sense of smell, to catch the green,
  Sun-ripened, rain-sweet smell of earth;
"Solo 3 (stronger):
  For eyes to see the colors blend,
  and splash with glory on the hill;
"1 and 2 (getting loud):
  For voice to speak, and shout and sing,
"1, 2 and 3: (leading to climax):
  Praise God from Whom all blessings flow,
  Praise Him all creatures here below,
  Praise Him above, ye heavenly host,
  Praise Father, Son, and Holy Ghost!" [3]

Suggestions for Discussion and Action:

It is the most natural thing in the world for man to praise God, to be aware of all that has been given to him. It is natural that the praise is also a form of thanksgiving.

From the earliest days man has given thanks—whether it be to God or to the Corn Spirit or to the Greek goddess Ceres—hoping that the spring will come after the winter and the crops will begin to grow. Today most people live in cities and are far removed from the seed and the harvest. Yet just as God taught man to till the land, grow fruit, or raise cattle, it is also God who gave man the brain to build the skyscrapers and the factories with the intricate machinery and flowing assembly lines.

Once man brought the first of his fruits or his finest work to the church at harvest time, but that idea is dying out. However, some churches have *industrial* harvest festivals! One church asked all the industry in the area to send samples to the church. (In some ways you could say it was like a Science Fair, with thanks to

God for man's ability to make the exhibits!) Yet the exhibits were not all of a technical nature. Even hat making and cake making were included.

This industrial exhibition and festival was open to the public all day Saturday and closed with a special service on Sunday evening. The minister who led the service said: *"This* Festival is a symbol of the church at work in a technological society.

"Computers instead of cucumbers, as it were. As all life belongs to God there is nothing incongruous about having ballbearings next to bread, thus introducing the modern workman's skill to the congregation. . . .

"God is Creator, and as managers and employers we have the privilege of being stewards of his creation." [4]

What does this say to us? Are we too inclined to praise and thank God only for the beautiful things we see in his world? What do we do with our own brains and hands, what do we create, or what do others in our group or church or community create for which we should offer praise and thanks to God?

Prayer:

Write your own this time: a prayer of praise and thanks for the specific things done among you all, in either work or leisure time. Be careful to avoid a prayer full of generalities. You might also want to add praise and thanks for fine work in industry or the arts by others in your church or community.

3. THE WONDERS OF GOD'S WORLD

Scripture: John 3:16, NEB ("God loved the world so much.")

Reading:

"The lesson for this Sunday morning in a certain city church was on "The Wonders of God's World." Although the children lived in the center of the city, most of them had managed to find something of nature's beauty to bring to class as the teacher had requested the previous Sunday. There was, for example, a beetle with green shine on its wings, some small yellow weed flowers, a rock with mica in it, and some large leaves from the trees on the housing project.

"As the session began Jessica and her little brother, Michael, were detached and quiet, their eyes solemn and troubled. All efforts of the teacher to involve them met with quiet stares. Finally, she sat down beside them while the others were arranging their exhibits.

" 'Couldn't you find anything to bring?' she asked quietly.

"Jessica did not answer that question. She said simply, 'A little baby fell out of the seventh-floor window in our building this morning. We saw it, it was dead.'

"Michael spoke up excitedly, 'It was all bloody.'

"Suddenly the day's session on 'The Wonders of God's World' blurred a little before the eyes of the teacher. The other children, hearing Michael's statement, came over to listen. The teacher was quiet a moment and then said, 'There are beautiful things in God's world, and there are also things that are sad and hard to understand. Often people are responsible for the sad and ugly things we find around us, but there are also accidents and people get hurt through no fault of their own, and are sometimes killed.'

"This started an excited recital of street accidents and fires witnessed by other children. Suddenly questions started coming, and for the time being the exhibits were forgotten. The stark realities of the daily life of the children became the focal point of interest. Because she was experienced, the teacher allowed the session to build upon the questions that came pouring forth. The wonders of God's world became the wonder of God's love in the midst of suffering, sorrow, and death. To have attempted to proceed with the lesson as planned would have resulted in a session completely irrelevant to those children at that time." [5]

Suggestions for Discussion and Action:

Read the suggested scripture again. How can we help people—and especially children—who have known and seen heartbreaking things to become aware of God's love that transcends all human sufferings?

It would be too easy to cut short our own spontaneous moments of praise and thanks to God for the wonder of his world, and scourge ourselves with the recollection of those who have little cause for spontaneous thanks.

It would be even easier to keep away from those who suffer, so that thought of them does not disturb our contemplation of a rose unfolding, or a gaggle of geese etched on a winter sky.

Pierre Teilhard de Chardin, the great Roman Catholic priest and paleontologist loved to quote a saying of Pierre Termier, "Everything that happens is adorable!" [6] What did he mean? What was his understanding of the word "adorable"? Have we the courage to find the way to praise and adore God in the unpleasant things that happen to us? If so, will it help us to help others when in trouble? Perhaps the key lies in something else Teilhard said, "If only men loved one another—in the context of something greater than themselves—how changed the world would be, how invincible and armed for every conquest." [7]

Relate this sentence to the story you have just heard. If this became reality, maybe the baby would not have fallen out of the window in the first place. To what degree are we responsible for what those two children saw? What are we doing about it?

What are you doing about it? Is your group working with loving concern among any who are less fortunate?

Prayer:

"Praise be to the God and Father of our Lord Jesus Christ, the all-merciful Father, the God whose consolation never fails us! He comforts us in all our troubles, so that we in turn may be able to comfort others in any trouble of theirs and to share with them the consolation we ourselves receive from God." Amen. (II Cor. 1:3-4, NEB.)

4. WHAT IS WORSHIP?

Scripture: Eph. 3:14-19, NEB

"I kneel in prayer to the Father, from whom every family in heaven and on earth takes its name, that out of the treasures of his glory he may grant you strength and power through his Spirit in your inner being, that through faith Christ may dwell in your hearts in love. With deep roots and firm foundations, may you be strong to grasp, with all God's people, what is the breadth and length and height and depth of the love of Christ, and to know it, though it is beyond knowledge."

Reading:

"What is Worship?

"Firstly and fundamentally, it is a human activity—the highest and most truly human of all men's actions. Worship is man's response to the gift of life. In worship we offer praise to God for all the wonder, the joy and the terror of life. Unless we see life as meaningless and without joy, we must see all creation as existing to the Glory of God. We see that it has a glory beyond all the uses that we may try to draw out of it. Man shares in this praise that all creation offers to God but does so in a unique way. His praise is conscious, deliberate and articulate. The worship of the Church is no less human. Indeed it is peculiarly human. It is the response of men to all that God has done for men in Christ. . . . Because worship is this human response to God's glory, there always occurs in true worship the meeting of the universal and eternal with the immediate and personal—God's glory and man's response. The glory to which worship is a response is so wide and so deep in human experience that it can never be expressed solely in words. It touches the whole of man's life. It has to be expressed, however inadequately, in all the creative responses of man's spirit—in music and in art, in social life and in sport. It belongs to all. And it issues in response—in the intentions and actions of men and women in their particular situations. In worship the eternal meets the immediate, the universal the particular. Worship becomes the motive power of the action of faith.

"Or it should. For if this were so, would worship today seem to so many to be remote and meaningless?" [8]

Suggestions for Discussion and Action:

The reading you have just heard is from an article written by T. R. Morton of the Iona Community in response to a youth leader who said that worship was for him the great difficulty in his work. He said he found it more difficult to work with young people inside the church, than outside, for this very reason.

Would you agree with him? Lead a discussion on worship today, and encourage everyone to speak freely. If there is criticism, is it of the worship of your own group, or of the corporate worship of the congregation?

Is the complaint obscurity of language or obscurity of meaning, leading to difficulty in real participation? Do you feel that worship is not sufficiently related to the lives of men in the world? Do you feel it should be? Why?

The reader said that "worship is man's response to the gift of life." What did he mean? What do you expect to give or take from participation in worship? Read the suggested scripture again, as a basis for thinking about this. "Worship, in the eyes of men today, has lost its scale of greatness, perhaps because men have lost any measure of greatness. It seems to have to do only with the private lives of men." [9] Worship should be in the plural. Why?

Do you try to find new prayers and hymns relevant to your lives today? Have you included art and drama?

Prayer:

"Almighty God, the bread we eat, and the roof which shelters us; the light of day which gives us sight, and the darkness of the night which grants us rest; the work of our hands, by which we humbly serve the world, and the dreams of our hearts which lure us to greater deeds; the accustomed things we have grown to know and love, and the bright invasion of new glory from unexpected sources—all these things, and more beside, praise thy name with thankfulness, through Jesus Christ, the Eternal Gift of thy goodness. Amen." [10]

5. THE MEANING OF HOLY COMMUNION

Scripture: Matt. 26:17-30 ("The Last Supper.")

Reading:

The sacrament of Holy Communion is the heart of all worship. It is a thing of absolute simplicity—"the taking, blessing, breaking and giving of bread and the taking, blessing and giving of a cup of wine and water, as these were first done with their new meaning by a young Jew before and after supper with His friends on the night before He died. Soon it was simplified still further, by leaving out the supper and combining the double grouping before and after it into a simple rite. So the four-action Shape of the liturgy was found by the end of the first century. . . .

"Was ever another command so obeyed? For century after century, spreading slowly to every continent and country and among every race on earth, this action has been done, in every conceivable human circumstance, for every conceivable human need from infancy and before it to extreme old age and after it, from the pinnacles of earthly greatness to the refuge of fugitives in the dens and caves of the earth. Men have found no better thing than this to do for kings at their crowning and for criminals going to the scaffold; for armies in triumph or for a bride and bridegroom in a little country church; for the proclamation of a dogma or for a good crop of wheat; for the wisdom of the Parliament of a mighty nation or for a sick old woman afraid to die; for a schoolboy sitting an examination or for Columbus setting out to discover America; for the famine of whole provinces or for the soul of a dead lover; in thankfulness because my father did not die of pneumonia; for a village headman much tempted to return to fetich because the yams had failed; because the Turk was at the gates of Vienna; for the repentance of Margaret; for the settlement of a strike; for a son for a barren woman; for captain so-and-so, wounded and prisoner of war; while the lions roared in the nearby amphitheatre; on the beach at Dunkirk, while the hiss of scythes in the thick June grass came faintly through the windows of the church; tremulously, by an old monk on the fiftieth anniversary of his vows; furtively by an exiled bishop who had hewn timber all day in a prison camp near Murmansk; gorgeously, for the canonization of S. Joan of Arc—one could fill many pages with the reasons why men have done this, and not tell a hundredth part of them." [11]

Suggestions for Discussion and Action:

What is this celebration which is at the heart of all worship? Some call it Holy Communion or the Lord's Supper. Some call it the Eucharist (from the Greek word "thanksgiving"). It is the time when we declare our union with Christ in the way he commanded us to do, offering the bread and wine created by the hands of men. In a ceremony in which everyone shares we receive the gift of renewal so that we may continue the ministry of Jesus Christ to the world, to love as we have been loved.

In the early days this was a communal meal which Christians shared every Sunday with great joy and thanksgiving. Bread and wine were basic elements of man's meal, as they still are in many countries of Southern Europe and the Middle East.

Has it stayed a simple, joyful, weekly occasion? No. Through the years, the Communion became steeped in more mysticism and more ceremony, with the tinkling of bells, odor of incense, and rustle of rich robes, while the congregation either watched, or felt that their part was a very humble one. With the coming of the Reformation, a great deal of the earlier simplicity was regained, but the service was austere and lacked the joy and spontaneity of the first Christians.

Today Holy Communion is becoming more a blend of what it used to be and what it should be in the contemporary world. In new buildings the altar is rarely fixed to the back wall. In some churches the table or altar (or whatever the denomination chooses to call it) is right in the center of the church so that everyone can gather round it. Not only that, Holy Communion is sometimes celebrated outside the church in the homes of the people. This has always been done for the sick and dying, but rarely for ordinary groups.

How is Holy Communion celebrated in the churches in your community? Why not visit some, especially if you know of any new buildings where the table is in the center.

Notice the different ways in which the sacrament is administered and the people receive it—different details in the interpretation of God's gift to his church everywhere, and in which all Christians are united.

Prayer:

"O God, to eat at thy table, is it not to be thy guest in an eternal kingdom of wonder and light? To partake of thy bread, is it not to be nurtured by the labor of the stars and earth, by subtle mysteries and unknown people? Is it not to share in the communion of that spirit by which the worlds were made and by which we are able to forget self in the company of others? Is it not to remember him, whose death revealed a glory no breaking of the body could destroy, a glory no condemnation could degrade, a glory no sorrow could extinguish? To eat and drink, that this humblest act of life might be glorified by the joys of the eternal soul, this we come to do, O God, in search of heaven's blessing. Amen." [12]

6. A TABLE WITH A ROOF OVER IT

Scripture: John 12:1-8 ("Why was this ointment not sold . . . and given to the poor?")

Reading:

What should a church building be like? The most magnificent work of art that man can assemble from out of his deep need to glorify God—or merely a "table with a roof over it"?

Is it true that the Communion table should be the central point in a church—the point which an architect keeps in mind when he begins to design a church, and not merely a necessary piece of furniture which he fits in somewhere as he plans a building that will be strikingly modern, split-level, ranch style, or just plain peculiar?

When Bishop Kilmer Myers spoke of the fact that a church building might one day become merely "a table with a roof over it" he was hoping that people would begin to see that worship is the primary activity of the church, and that the primary activity of the pastor or minister or priest is the serving of Holy Communion with the people gathered round a simple table to receive it, before going out to "become the cutting edge of the church in the world." [13]

Today, the gathered people of God who are the church are beginning to do this more and more. Ministers are also turning more and more to serve in industry, hospitals, slums, universities, and situations where there is no formal church building. So there are bound to be those who say, "Why do we need church buildings at all? They are a waste of money!"

Man has a deep need to glorify God in some special place, sanctified for that purpose. A place of beauty, the work of fine artists, where those who are not artists themselves can share in their forms of creativity which glorify God—be they stonecutters, glassworkers, woodworkers, painters, metalworkers, or musicians. But there can be danger in too much art for art's sake! A young

American visited a Russian Orthodox Church in Kiev. He said: "The music carries you into another world. Time stands still. One's heart soars as the priest, the deacons and the choirs sing prayers of praise, thanksgiving, suffering, penitence, forgiveness and grace. The faces of the worshipers shine with devotion. The eyes of the priest burn with passion. The triumphant beauty of the singing is matched by the splendor and pathos of the ikons. The priest and four or five deacons in resplendent robes of gold, green, blue and white march in and out of the *bema*, carrying the Bible, chanting and enacting the drama of the mass.

"Yet this is not merely an aesthetic experience. Once when I was looking up at the ikons on the ceiling of a church in Kiev, a young man behind me tapped my shoulder and said, 'You are disturbing the worship; this is not a museum!' " [14]

We need to remember this too!

So what are we looking for? A building of simple beauty, where the Communion table is central to the entire architectural scheme. A building that is not so blatantly extravagant and expensive that the unbeliever will laugh when he hears of the church's mission to the poor, the sick, and the fainthearted.

"The English Prayer Book requires that the bread which is used at the Eucharist shall be 'the best and purest . . . that conveniently may be gotten.' " [15] This maxim could be applied to all that is related to a church building.

Suggestions for Discussion and Action:

Read the suggested scripture again. Why do you think it was chosen?

At what times do we want to give all that we have? Where does wise judgment come into the picture?

What do the church buildings you know say of the people who built or use them? Apart from the Communion table or altar, what other factors, objects, and layouts are needed for a church to be a church? What do churches have today that they did not have fifty years ago? And vice versa?

Someone once said that the first thing an unbeliever ought to say when he sees a church is, "There men meet with God," and then, "Come in." [16] This is all very well, but today we want a church that gives the impression that people will come bursting out of it into the world too! How can we do that? (Not through a mere building, but by remembering that the people *are* the church, and are known by what they do in the world.)

At one time the church was the heart of the city. All life was tied to it, and we need to remember that all art, music, schools, and even hospitals began under the hand of the church. The church *was* the community. John Osman has said, "It is proper that the Temple and the Cathedral should be the prevailing forms against the skylines of man's towns and cities. Old Trinity Church at the entrance to Wall Street and St. Patrick's Cathedral set against Rockefeller Plaza are parables of the ways of men in cities." [17]

He feels that perhaps we need religious centers to pick up the religious life which is lying around in pieces in the city. Do we need a religious center like Lincoln Square Center for the Performing Arts, or Rockefeller Plaza, or the United Nations Plaza? (But not like those at the New York World's Fair!) After all, we have them for everything else, from medicine to groceries. John Osman looks on a religious center as "a sanctuary for a whole city. Yet it stands in judgment over the city. It is *prophetic* as well as *sacramental*." [18] What do you think?

Prayer:

O God, may we someday take part in the building of a church worthy of thy glory, and may we be worthy of that church. Amen.

ADDITIONAL WORSHIP RESOURCES

Scripture:

I Chron. 29:10-13 ("Thine, O Lord, is the greatness, and the power, and the glory.")

Ps. 34:1-3 ("O magnify the Lord with me.")
Ps. 96:1-6 ("Declare his glory among the nations.")
Ps. 100 ("Serve the Lord with gladness.")
Isa. 6:1-8 ("Holy, holy, holy is the Lord of hosts.")
Jer. 9:23-24 ("Let not the wise man glory in his wisdom.")
Rom. 11:33-36 ("To him be glory forever.")
Eph. 3:20-21 ("To him be glory in the church.")
Rev. 4 ("Receive glory and honor and power.")
Rev. 5:11-14 ("To him . . . be . . . honor and glory and might
        for ever and ever!")

Prayer:

This is a prayer for Christmas Day, written by Bishop Ken, who lived in the seventeenth century. It is included here as a classic example of man's joy as he contemplates God's glory.

"Glory be to God in the highest, and on earth peace, good will towards men: for unto us is born this day a Saviour, Who is Christ the Lord. We praise Thee, we bless Thee, we glorify Thee, we give thanks unto Thee, for this greatest of Thy mercies, O Lord God, Heavenly King, God the Father Almighty. O Lord, the only begotten Son Jesus Christ, O Lord God, Lamb of God, Son of the Father, Who wast made man to take away the sins of the world, have mercy upon us by turning us from our iniquities. Thou Who wast manifested to destroy the works of the devil, have mercy upon us by enabling us to renounce and forsake them. Thou Who art the great Advocate with the Father, receive our prayer, we humbly beseech Thee. Amen."

> "Deep peace of the running wave to you,
>   Deep peace of the flowing air to you,
>   Deep peace of the quiet earth to you,
>   Deep peace of the shining stars to you,
>   Deep peace of the watching shepherds to you,
>   Deep peace of the Son of Peace to you." [19]

"At the Yale University commencement service during which President John F. Kennedy received an honorary degree, Yale Chaplain, William Sloane Coffin, gave the following prayer:

'For glimpses of beauty, for hours of truth, for tastes of justice and the feel of freedom, for music and mirth, for love and laughter, Lord, we love thy world, this nation and this place.

'Because we love the world we pray now, O Father, for grace to quarrel with it, O Thou whose lover's quarrel with the world is the history of the world. Grant us grace to quarrel with the worship of success and power, with the assumption that people are less important than the jobs they hold. Grant us grace to quarrel with a mass culture that tends not to satisfy but to exploit the wants of people; to quarrel with those who pledge allegiance to one race rather than the human race; and with those who prefer to condemn communism rather than to practice Christianity. Lord, grant us grace to quarrel with all that profanes and trivializes and separates men.

'Number us, we beseech thee, in the ranks of those who went forth from this university longing only for those things for which thou dost make us long; men for whom the complexity of issues only served to renew their zeal to deal with them; men who alleviated pain by sharing it; and men who were always willing to risk something big for something good.

'So may we leave in the world a little more truth, a little more justice, a little more beauty than would have been there had we not loved the world enough to quarrel with it for what it is not but could be. O God, take our minds and think through them; take our lips and speak through them; and take our hearts and set them on fire. Amen.' " [20]

Hymns:

Joyful, Joyful, We Adore Thee
Praise the Lord: Ye Heavens Adore Him
Lord, Thy Glory Fills the Heaven

All Creatures of Our God and King
Let All the World in Every Corner Sing
Holy, Holy, Holy! Lord God Almighty
Honor and Glory, Power and Salvation
Ancient of Days Who Sittest Throned in Glory
Praise to the Lord, the Almighty, the King of Creation!
Immortal, Invisible, God Only Wise

chapter IX

OPPORTUNITIES FOR ACTION BY
COMFORTABLE CHRISTIANS

Geddes MacGregor has said that the people should be called to worship, not by "the sweet nothings that are sometimes langourously purled on a carillon," but by "three sharp blasts on a factory whistle." [1]

We gather together in worship for renewal and preparation for going back to work as part of the church in the world, but here, also, the benediction used at the close of most Protestant services has a soothing sound. How much better is the "Ite!" pronounced at the end of a Roman Catholic service, which means, "Go out into the world!"

What *are* we doing out in the world?

What action is needed?

The youth of today are tired of "churchy" programs led by "churchy" leaders, whose aim seems to be to collect a group of "nice" young people within the comfortable security of a church building.

The Methodist Youth Fellowship expressed this feeling quite forcibly at its National Conference in 1963. They spoke for the youth of most denominations when they drew up a document that said:

"Because we believe that there is a crashing need for youth to be able to experience what it means to be the church in the world at this moment; because youth need to respond to the gospel as a full member of the body of Christ rather than as participants in an established pattern of organization;

"Because we believe that the demands of the gospel are met through study, prayer, action, and conversation about the Christian faith, life, and mission; and that the needs of the world are met in the world:

"Therefore, we propose that for two years the National Conference of the Methodist Youth Fellowship direct its energies toward providing special opportunities for youth to grow in their understanding of what it means to be the church." [2]

This chapter contains accounts of many exciting and vital ways in which youth are showing "their understanding of what it means to be the church." Maybe they will stimulate you to have fresh ideas of your own. You will also find information and addresses of opportunities for action in which your group, or individuals, could participate. The question is not "Are you interested?" but "What will you choose to do?" as you share in the renewal of the church in the world.

ACTION IN THE WORLD TODAY

Intentional Communities.

These projects are sponsored by the National Conference of the Methodist Youth Fellowship, mentioned above. Intentional communities are held in various locations—day camps, housing projects, coffeehouses—where youths and adults can practice existing as the church in the world. Two persons may be employed to earn money to support the community, with six participating in voluntary service jobs. Emphasis is made upon a disciplined community life characterized by study and worship together. Conversation is apt to be on what each has found it like to be the church in secular society.

Participants pay their own transportation, but living costs are provided for the ten weeks by the community.

The Catacomb.

This is a place where teenagers "hang out" in an industrial city in Scotland. It was one of the first experiments of taking the church out to meet young people where they are. Started in 1959 in a few rooms loaned by the Bathgate YMCA, it now resounds with pop music at full volume, the confusion of jive and talk in an atmosphere that is cheerful and relaxed. Young people from the several church groups behind it are on good terms with those who are, perhaps "on probation," who swagger in, or the "wise guys" with attention-provoking outfits. There are no membership dues, nothing to make anyone feel inferior, no one insisting on a sermon or a little evangelism when the opportunity might arise.

Sometimes there are discussions that generate of their own accord. Sometimes a few newspaper clippings about a race riot, or pictures of refugees and starving children will start questions.

One of the organizers of The Catacomb said, "Would to God, that we had more young folk who were prepared to venture as these from Bathgate have done, to new ways of service. The Youth Fellowships and the Church in general need a new reforming spirit, which will take us all out of our ivory castles, contented, smug and self satisfied, into the Catacombs where new life is thriving and throbbing." [3] Perhaps the most significant comment came from a boy who said to a girl who belonged to one of the church youth fellowships, "Och, dinna worry aboot that—we dinna haud it against ye!" [4]

Encounter.

Encounter is a coffeehouse lay center in downtown Lancaster, Pennsylvania. It is supported by thirty-four congregations of the

United Church of Christ. The store front building has a coffee bar, tables, chairs, pictures, sculpture, books, and magazines. It is open seven to twelve hours a day, five days a week and is staffed by one or two at the coffee urn (from a seventy-five member "lay corps" or volunteers).

Who comes? The unemployed, the old, the artist, the teenager, the welfare worker, the college student. There is much talk over many cups of coffee, and the "lay corpsman on duty has to remind himself then that the silent testimony of simply being there and available is the word that the world is hearing—a word that shatters the widespread belief that the church does not really care about the Jericho roads that honeycomb the metropolis." [5]

When a good movie comes to town, signs go up in the theater, inviting the public to come over afterwards and discuss it with a cup of coffee. Signs in hotels, bowling alleys, taverns, cafés, and church buildings give notice of special events, art exhibits, courses led by college and seminary faculty on contemporary literature and drama, Bible and theology. Forums are held, led by national leaders, perhaps on civil rights or local problems.

All kinds of people who would never set foot in a church, come and participate.

This is not a youth project, but one in which Christian youth of today can participate.

Coffeehouse on Campus.

Ichthus Coffeehouse is at the University of Texas, in the Methodist Student Center. It is simply a place where there is no hurry, no push, but a chance to visit and talk about anything. A few students are chosen and trained to chat with those who are there, but without using the traditional jargon of the Christian faith. There is a low key program for about ten to fifteen minutes once an hour on the hour.

The only worship held is among the group operating the Coffee House, speakers for the evening, etc.

Coffeehouses Lead Opinion.

After the race riots in New York in the summer of 1964, a committee representing forty-seven Protestant and Roman Catholic churches began a $100,000 crash program to provide jobs, training, and recreation for Negro youths. More than six hundred boys and girls were hired to renovate church property, work on voter registration, clear yards and playgrounds, and assist handicapped and elderly people. Many more were in Summer workshops and camps and participated in coffeehouse sessions, plays, dances, and other cultural events.

Program and activities were based on suggestions made in forums in the coffeehouses!

Youth for Service, San Francisco.

Teen-age gangs have been turned into self-governing youth clubs. The social program goes along with service projects which have included cleaning up and repairing a nursery school and escorting residents of a home for aged women on sightseeing trips.

Young people in the churches in some areas have taken on jobs. Oakland's united Christian youth council collected ten thousand pounds of clothing for Church World Service. Another group raised money to send underprivileged Indian children to church-sponsored camps. Others have led special training in how to visit people and formed teams to visit shut-ins or elderly people.

One Night Stand Coffeehouse.

At a youth rally for Presbyterian senior highs the hall was filled with many card tables, each with a candle in a coke bottle, cloths of construction paper, and a few crayons scattered invitingly about. Young people from the host church sold pop and potato chips. The walls were decorated with newspapers and some art exhibits. The whole atmosphere was designed to provide a setting for stimulating conversation, and everyone was urged to ask questions and present his own views frankly. There was a short program of original poetry, drama, and folk songs, as well as some interesting art work on the table cloths!

It was hard to create the relaxed atmosphere of an established coffeehouse, but it gave many young people an idea of what they are like, and perhaps made them contemplate having one in their own community.

Festival Night Club.

During the summer, Edinburgh is "cultural host to some 80,000 visitors from all parts of the world. Beyond an opening gesture in St. Giles there has been little positive indication that the Church has involved itself or that it has any relevant message or concern for Festival Visitors. . . . A small beginning was made towards Youth through Cephas, the youth rendezvous in the basement of St. George's West Church, Edinburgh.

"Helped by members of Youth Fellowships from all over Edinburgh, . . . our subterranean crypt became a Festival Night Club with a difference. We met Christians from many parts of the world and to them and all our visitors we trust Cephas was a place of warmth and friendliness.

"This year we are repeating our club. The Crypt—last year a Baronial Hall—is an Hebridean Island with crofts, one for a display of Scottish Crafts with pottery making, etc., another exhibiting Scottish Paintings and projecting slides of the Highlands to a background of lilting music and another, the interior of a Fisherman's Shieling. Our menu, of course, is Scottish fare with porridge, haggis, partridge, soup, etc.

"The programme of entertainment is varied and ambitious from Folk Singing to Jazz, with raconteurs, Pipers, Highland Dancers, etc., with opportunity to join in.

"Every evening, as always in Cephas, we have the privilege of speaking for Christ and in our Chapel Service of Worship and discussion together.

"From all countries we worship together each Sunday evening before the club opens, from 8:30-9 p.m.; the services respectively incorporating International Christian folk music, the Lord's Supper and the modern drama of the death of Christ 'A Man Dies.' " [6]

Operation Cleanup.

Bethlehem Church, Minneapolis, is in an area crowded with rooming houses and apartments, overflowing with six thousand young adults who have come to the city to work or study. The church had a good program for them, but was in desperate need of a cheerful neighborhood recreation center.

Senior highs of another church, Westminster, had been looking for a work project. They volunteered to renovate the drab basement of the Bethlehem church. This took several Saturdays of hard work. Each Friday night the *boys* showed up in Bethlehem's kitchen to prepare the food for the next day! "Operation Cleanup" was a big success, with everything planned the day before, and many of Bethlehem's young adults helped too.

Pick and Shovel Fellowship.

A few years ago in France a group of people began making a parking lot for a church. The boys loosened up the dirt with picks; the girls shoveled it away in wheelbarrows. As they worked, they talked, and it was fascinating talk. Three were expriests, one a math professor, one a conscientious objector, one a theological student whose wife was there too. American, French, Dutch, Hungarian— they were all part of an international work camp. They shared KP duty, worshiped, and studied together. This was an Ecumenical Voluntary Service Project, sponsored by the World Council of Churches.

In the summer of 1964 one thousand students served programs in twenty-six countries—laying out a street in Germany; working with farm laborers in Holland; working on a school in Ghana, a church in Belgium, a road in Japan—without pay and paying their own transportation.

Wanted Volunteers.

Volunteers served three days a week for four weeks at a camp for handicapped children in Allentown, Pennsylvania. JoAnn Chisholm, seventeen, was an instructor in arts and crafts and loved it. The volunteers taught music, dramatics, and nature study. They also had a hootenanny and a mock circus. "I never expected camp to be so much fun. The boys and girls are full of enthusiasm and want to be on the go every minute. When we play hide-and-seek, the crutches and wheelchairs fly by in an attempt to tag home first." [7]

Any Crippled Children's Society can give information to those who want to be counselors.

Letter from London, England.

"I have volunteered to do part of the organization of The London Young Friends Work Camps. We do various kinds of volunteer weekend work, my job being to find exactly what work. There is normally one camp a month, attended by 6-20 people; usually about half are Quakers. "Camp" means camp beds and sleeping bags, in a Meeting House, Church Hall, or something. We are quite often joined by about 3 prisoners, on parole from Wandsworth (prison) in the morning, and take them back in the evening.

"Jobs are highly variable, but this year's programme seems to be fairly representative. October: Tidying up the garden of Uxbridge Meeting House. November, December: Decorating for old people in Hammersmith, Streatham Camp—about 6 rooms. January, April: tree planting and felling in the Chiltern Hills. February: Organizing a party and outing for the Balham and Tooting International Circle—largely foreign students. March: Decorating in the new Friends International Centre. May: Decorating at the Stepney Family Service Unit, club rooms. June: decorating for various people in the Islington area.

"We pay our own food and accommodation costs, but the FSU pays for materials we use. The FSUs deal with a small number of hopeless families in their areas—there are 14 in England, with about 75 families each, which have been given up as hopeless by the other Welfare organizations. I went to the Stepney Unit's Children's Camp last summer, and last November I took on an evening club of 4 boys. We meet for an hour and a half, once a week, in the basement of the Unit.

"The oldest boy is very dense, the next is above average in intelligence, and the other two are very bright. This makes it hard to get the oldest to join in anything—he's 12—but he likes to play the gramophone. The others play football, paint (themselves and the floor as much as the paper), and table tennis. There is a great deal of messing about, and we have a thick large mat which they can use for wrestling, handstands, etc. Because of the mat, shoes are usually off but they keep their socks on and must get them in a horrible state. I take mine off, but have a hard time getting the jam off my feet afterwards!" [8]

A Summer in San Francisco.

A group of college-age students went to San Francisco for what was called a "crash program," that lasted for seven weeks. They lived in Hospitality House, in the heart of the city's Mission District. A cook prepared their lunch and supper, but they had to fix their own breakfasts and meals over the weekends and share in the housekeeping.

First week: Orientation, when they learned about the jobs they would have to do and of the problems of the inner city.

Second and third weeks: They organized recreation in parks and streets closed off for the purpose. Five thousand doorknob hangers in all neighborhoods told children which of the eleven locations would be nearest to them.

Fourth and fifth weeks: They provided most of the leadership in six Daily Vacation Church Schools.

Sixth and seventh weeks: They took part in a program called "Exploring San Francisco," taking groups of children on trips to places of interest.

While doing all this, they also worked on an "adult leadership survey" in a large public housing area, searching for a responsible neighborhood citizen's committee from among the Negroes who lived there. *And* they did some calling for voter's registration too, as well as taking part in a demonstration!

Finally, they split into visitation teams, spending a weekend with a more affluent suburban congregation, talking to the young people there, and taking a major part in leading the Sunday morning worship when they spoke of their work.

They had Bible study and discussion, heard special speakers, and worshiped together every morning, but there was recreation too! A trip to a Pacific beach, a dinner, two visits to special drama performances, and time for exploring and recreation on their own.

This was called a "crash program," as the activities attracted many children who had no previous connection with the church. Regular workers contacted their families, after the students had gone.

Quite a way to spend a summer!

Australia's Christian Cabaret.

A few years ago the Central Methodist Mission in Sydney began a controversial teen-age cabaret. Held on Saturday nights, the program, with its modern rhythm music has attracted a hundred thousand teenagers since it began.

Young people rebel against the more traditional forms of church music, but respond to their own fast rhythms. Music is provided by a four-piece band, with popular vocalists. Some religious numbers are included, and sometimes traditional hymns are used with modern tunes, such as "Christ the Lord Is Risen Today" to the tune of "Michael Row the Boat Ashore."

The Reverend Alan Walker, who could be called the Billy Graham of Australia, gives an address, and many young people make their personal commitment to Christ.

At the heart of the cabaret there is a group of Christian young people, at least fifty of whom are on duty every night. They meet for worship first, and then go into the streets, milk bars, and hotels to invite youth to the cabaret.

This cabaret has certainly reestablished contact between the church and the masses of modern young people. The next problem is how to lead them into the Christian life in a church—and what *should* that be for this generation?

A Great Cathedral and Youth Today.

Coventry Cathedral is known the world over as a magnificent building to which scores of artists gave of their best. It is known as a center for reconciliation, but also as an international center for youth. A youth hostel is being built, which will house thirty young people. They spend the weekend at the Cathedral, taking part in its work and worship, and learning of the work of the church in a modern city. Some are involved in projects of music, art, and drama, especially at Christmas.

Unattached young people who live in Coventry have a lunch-time club, and many young people help the Cathedral staff, as guides to the thousands of visitors, or assist in the book store.

Project Applebutter.

Young people from a Church of God congregation in rural Virginia made applebutter! The farmers let the young people pick the surplus apples that did not get to market. They picked hundreds of bushels and spent hours mashing, peeling, and coring the apples. On the final day they began at 4:00 A.M., building fires under old-fashioned iron kettles. After being stirred thoroughly, the applebutter turned out so well that a local grocer bought the lot.

Purpose? To raise money so that the young people could attend their national youth conference, and to help some enroll in their denominational college.

After Mississippi, Summer 1964.

Cynthia Small was among the many students and adults who went to Mississippi to work on voter registration. She wrote about two women whose attitude to the problem of hate and violence there made her think about the basic problem of inherent evil in a way she had never done before. These two women believed in the fundamental goodness of all human beings, and that those who were responsible for the murder of the three white men merely needed someone to reach out to the goodness in them.

This concerned Cynthia Small, and she began to think of the instances of violence and hate she came across herself, and talked to others about it. She wrote about the two women: "Could it not be that they were leaving out a very important part of the picture by not recognizing the existence of an evil, of evil in individuals themselves, perhaps an evil as basic as the good? . . . And may not the visible mixture of good and evil in Mississippi be a sign of a similar condition in the soul of all humanity?" [9]

These thoughts will plague all those who go out to work for and love their neighbor, no matter who or where he is. Is nonviolence always the answer?

Operation Reconciliation (Aktion Suhnezeichen).

This is a volunteer project sponsored by Germany's Protestant Church to rebuild where Nazi troops had destroyed. Young people seventeen to twenty-five years old, students and craftsmen, give up about six months of their time to go to other countries and build churches, homes, youth centers. Expenses are covered by individuals, congregations, and civic groups. The Netherlands, Norway, Greece, France, even Israel have been helped. Eleven were allowed to go to the Urin *Kibbutz*—a nurse, a secretary, an electrician, a tinsmith, a stenographer, a parish worker, a farmer, a catechist, a kindergarten teacher, a student, and one older man—a minister.

"Said an orthodox Jew from Jerusalem with tears in his eyes: 'When one person says to another, "I would like to love you," one is glad. But when this is said by a person at whose hands one has suffered, there is no greater joy.' " [10]

There was earlier mention of the sixteen young Germans who helped rebuild Coventry Cathedral. Now funds are being raised for similar aid *to* Germany, to build an extension to the church hospital at Dresden—a city badly damaged by Allied air raids.

Nes Ammim, Haifa, Israel

Nes Ammim has been called a "bridge between Christians and Jews." It will be a village surrounded by about 260 acres of good land to raise the usual crops and eventually citrus trees and bananas.

International and interdenominational workers will live in the village-community, which will have living-barracks, dining hall, kitchen, workshop, activity room, school, etc.

The president of the US-NES AMMIM committee is Addison J. Eastman, 475 Riverside Drive, New York, New York 10027.

Churches Look at One Another.

Young people (all attending the same high school) from about five churches met for a weekend to look at their common faith in the world of the high school they share. This was led by the Episcopal Church, and is now being done in other communities too.

City Country Swap.

Young people from a church in Maine have exchanged visits, with a large Presbyterian church in New York City. Each group stayed in the homes of church families, and saw the "sights"— Empire State Building, Radio City Music Hall, etc., in the city; and farms, a corn-canning factory, ski tow, and beautiful forests and rolling hills in Maine. They compared their work, lives, and worship.

Adults and Senior Highs on Retreat Together.

When a church in New York state began to make plans for its annual adult retreat, the senior highs asked if they could take part too. They had heard of new directions in youth work, wanted to discuss them with adult leaders in their church, and perhaps try some of them out. They were invited, and the venture was a big success, to be repeated every year from now on. Worth trying?

City Farmers.

The Robert R. Taylor homes, Chicago, the world's largest housing project has more than half of its 29,000 tenants on relief. Fifty parents have been given plots of land in nearby Gary, Indiana, where they can raise their own vegetables. The idea was thought up by the Firman House Community center which has provided six acres for this "farming." Three times a week the families commute to Gary. They have developed a new trade through it, for the excess produce is sold locally. Local funds have paid for seed, equipment, and the bus that transports them from Chicago.

A brand new project in its first year! What will it lead to? In how many places could it be copied?

Sunday on Wednesday.

A Presbyterian church in downtown Sydney, Australia, holds a worship service at noon on Wednesdays. One thousand fill the church, and hundreds of others watch the service on closed-circuit TV. The services are also broadcast over twenty-one radio stations.

Faith in Life Experiment.

The American Lutheran Church held a week-long conference in Fargo, North Dakota, and Moorhead, Minnesota, in 1964. The idea was to get people talking about their faith out in the community. In some ways it resembled the German Kirchentag. Religious leaders kept in the background, but sponsored two hundred talks. Special discussion-provoking movies like *Becket* and *Black Like Me* were shown in local movie houses. Neighborhood get-togethers were planned in connection with it, and people of all ages and all denominations made it a great success. So much so that another conference is planned next year, in Duluth. It

made people feel that it was all right to talk about religion anywhere and that religion *belonged* anywhere.

Maundy Thursday Service in East Harlem

"The discovery of the power of community has come as we have
been able to develop forms of worship in our services of Holy
Communion that are genuine reminders of the worship of the
early church. They help us in our imaginations to live more fully
in the knowledge of the mighty acts of God. On last Maundy
Thursday, for example, we removed the pews from the front of
the church and put in long wooden tables. At 8:30 in the evening
the congregation gathered for worship, sitting around the tables
while the church officers and ministers gathered around the communion table in the chancel. We shared a fellowship meal of bread,
wine, and fish during which we talked with one another and sang
hymns. Following the meal one of the ministers, standing in the
center of the congregation, preached a sermon on the servant Lord
and servant people, explaining the nature of our servanthood in
Christ. Then the clergy, kneeling on the front steps of the chancel, wiped one by one the shoes of the members of the congregation,
using one end of the stole. After this they returned to their places
at the communion table and the bread was then passed from hand
to hand around the tables, and likewise the cup." [11]

The Loft.

Is there not some relationship between this Maundy Thursday
action, and the coffee shop in Burlington, Vt. where the minister
serves once a week as a waiter?

Waiters who are laymen from the sponsoring Presbyterian
church serve the people also. Monthly meetings are held. Menu
changes and kitchen procedures are worked out. Then significant
encounters and experiences are discussed, for many people with
serious problems will visit "The Loft" repeatedly, and it is important that the "collective ministries" have continuity.

This church has a unique ministry, for there is no church building! "The Loft" sells paperback books (some two thousand titles) and schedules programs on sexual promiscuity, peace movements, right-wing movements, hallucinatory drugs, existentialism, politics, race relations, folk music, wire-tapping, modern art, book and film censorship, etc.

A motion picture has been made of this experiment in the mission of the church. It was taken from the TV program series, "Look Up and Live." (For more information see "Films on Church Renewal," p. 234.)

Kirkridge.

In 1964 John Oliver Nelson resigned his position as a professor at Yale Divinity School, to devote all his time to Kirkridge, as he felt there was a greater need for him there.

What is Kirkridge? It calls itself "a Christian group under discipline, a retreat-and-study center in the Pennsylvanian Appalachians, and a movement for power within the Church." A movement for power it surely must be, for some 1,800 men and women, clergy and laymen, go to this 320-acre mountain retreat every year.

What do they do there? The leaders aim "to confront seeking Christians with gifted leaders and with each other; to explore silence and liturgy; the arts and social imperatives; to enable a small covenanted circle to know koinonia afresh; above all to praise and acknowledge God as modern believers know him." Some of these "occasions," as they are called, are for special groups, but anyone is eagerly invited to attend the others. Subjects run from "Mothers and Their Ministry," "Scientists, Doctors and the New Age," "Dance, Drama and Liturgy," to "Retreat for Square-peg Seminarians"!

So far, there have been no "occasions" for youths—except those who happen to attend one on a special vocation, such as nursing, but many college students and seminarians attend.

A Vital Program for Youth.

This involves young people of high school and college age, and is held at The Ecumenical Institute, Chicago. Weekend seminars are held and are combinations of study on the wonder and serious-ness of being and doing in the twentieth-century world, well mixed with conversations, creative recreation, and experimental worship. This is no local project, students fly in from all parts of America, and the Institute is known throughout the world. Write for infor-mation to 3444 Congress Parkway, Chicago, Illinois 60624.

What Do We Know About Peace Education?

This is a major concern of the American Friends Service Com-mittee, which puts special emphasis on the Quaker testimony of peace. Regional speakers are available for discussions and con-ferences, as well as national seminars for high school students. For example, a recent topic was "The World's Isms: Capitalism, Com-munism, Fascism and Socialism." Perhaps the most well known work of the AFSC is their worldwide program of voluntary service by young people, some for as long as two years. Write for more information to 160 North 15th St., Philadelphia, Penn. 19102.

Ever Seen a Copy of "High Issues"?

It is a newssheet for high school students, put out by the Fel-lowship of Reconciliation, an organization also dedicated to peace among men. It is a single sheet and free (but contributions sure help)! What is it about? You might call it a "stirrer-upper." An excerpt here, a quotation that's apt, an account of what some young people are doing in the way of action and service. It is intended to stir you up, make you think, make you feel you are not doing anything that amounts to much. You might want to write for a few sample copies to FOR, Box 271, Nyack, N.Y.

WHAT CAN YOU DO?

So many young people take part in service projects every sum-mer that they almost form a Peace Corps of their own!

Some are in work camps, in the country, in the city, among those of different races, some study at conferences or take part in special projects and seminars. Some go overseas, and many of these are gone for several months or even a few years. Usually they get room and board, perhaps a small allowance for personal expenses. Nearly always they are responsible for their own transportation to the work center or starting place. Sometimes financial help can be given, and sometimes the local church can help.

This movement of young people out into the world to be of service is growing so fast that, in voluntary work camps alone, more than two million participated in 1963!

First of All Find Out What Your Denomination Offers!

Get a copy of *Invest Your Summer!* Every church should own an annual copy of *Invest Your Summer,* the catalog of service opportunities published by The Commission on Youth Service Projects.[12] This will tell you how you can go to Alaska to do construction work; process materials for Church World Service; help emotionally disturbed or crippled children in camps; work with the migrant children; work in the inner-city recreation centers; work for a year in Africa or Asia; go as a Winant volunteer to work in youth clubs in England, with a week on Iona; be part of the National Parks Ministry; or take part in an International Christian Youth Exchange.

What Are the Requirements?

"You must be willing to accept the discipline of your job. You are grateful *if* any free time is to be found—you need to bring patience to continue in the face of small response and the understanding needed to work diligently at a task that may fail. . . .

"You must be willing to share fully in the life of a group based on the thesis that the revelation of God through Christ makes sense in the 20th century." [13]

Perhaps You Cannot Leave Home . . .

What about volunteering in the evening where you live and work? The National Student Association and the Northern Student Movement plan tutorial projects in major cities across the country through which individuals may serve one or more evenings each week—helping children in their school work. Write to NSA, 3457 Chestnut Street, Philadelphia, Pennsylvania 19104, or NSM Box 404a Yale Station, New Haven, Connecticut.

Within your own community you may find, or could help organize, a Youth Employment Service, work in a hospital as an aide or "candy-striper," or help the sick or aged. Start looking for areas of need, and you will find so many things to do that you will not know what to choose!

If you cannot serve in a work camp overseas, you can help those who do—through the International Student Movement for the United Nations. There is a Gift Coupon scheme, whereby you choose a group you want to know and help, and raise or donate money for Gift Coupons (or sell UNESCO Gift Stamps). Write for all the details to Gift Coupons, United Nations Headquarters, New York, N.Y. 10017.

OTHER USEFUL ADDRESSES

American Friends Service Committee, 160 N. 15th Street, Philadelphia 2, Pennsylvania.

Council on Student Travel, Inc., 777 U. N. Plaza, New York, New York 10007.

International Christian Youth Exchange, 475 Riverside Drive, New York, New York 10027.

National Council of Churches, Christian Ministry in the National Parks, 475 Riverside Drive, New York, New York 10027.

World Council of Churches, apply to: Ecumenical Voluntary Service, room 753, 475 Riverside Drive, New York, New York 10027.

Winant Volunteers, Inc., Mrs. Matson, 865 Madison Avenue, New York, New York 10021.

YMCA National Council, Mr. Clarence Elliott, 291 Broadway, New York, New York 10007.

YWCA National Student Council, Miss Jean Whittet, 600 Lexington Ave., New York, New York 10022.

Anti-Defamation League of B'Nai B'rith, 315 Lexington Ave., New York, New York 10016

Office of Migrant Work, National Council of Churches, 475 Riverside Drive, New York, New York 10027.

Church World Service, 637 West 125th Street, New York, New York 10027.

East Harlem Protestant Parish, 2050 Second Avenue, New York, New York 10029.

Chicago Missionary Society, 2016 West Evergreen, Chicago, Illinois.

Department of International Affairs, National Council of Churches, 475 Riverside Drive, New York, New York, 10027.

CARE Packages, New York, New York 10016

Coordination Committee for International Voluntary Workcamps, 6 rue Franklin, Paris 16e, France.

NOTES

INTRODUCTION

1. From a news item in *The Christian Century*, September 9, 1964, p. 1115.
2. East Harlem Protestant Parish Newsletter, November, 1961.
3. If you are interested in new hymns, see the list of publications by The American Hymn Society, p. 234.

CHAPTER I

1. William Stringfellow, "The Secret of Christian Unity," in *The Christian Century*, September 13, 1961, p. 1073. Copyright 1961 Christian Century Foundation. Reprinted by permission from *The Christian Century*.
2. *Ibid.*, p. 1075-76.
3. *God's Frozen People* by Mark Gibbs and T. Ralph Morton. Philadelphia: The Westminster Press, 1965.
4. George Hunt, reprinted from *Today*, November-December, 1960. Copyright 1960 by W. L. Jenkins. Used by permission.
5. Sheila D. Woods, "Think of a Church . . . Our Church," in the *International Journal of Religious Education*, September, 1962, pp. 35-36.
6. Mark Gibbs, "Do You Have to Go to Church to Be a Christian?" in *Christian Comment*, June, 1963, pp. 1-4. Used by permission.
7. "God Roars in the Pines," in *Together*, September, 1960, p. 26.
8. "Why I Go to Church," in *Together*, September, 1961, pp. 13-14.

9. *Ibid.*, pp. 15-16.

10. John Wesley.

11. *Ausgewahlte Werke. Calwer Ausgabe*, 5, 154.

12. W. A. Visser 't Hooft, *The Renewal of the Church* (Philadelphia: The Westminster Press, 1956), p. 91.

13. Virginia L. Harbour, "A Platform for Youth Work," in *International Journal of Religious Education*, March, 1964, p. 8. Used by permission.

14. Adapted from the *Book of Common Order*. Found in the brochure published to commemorate the dedication of Kildrum Parish Church.

15. From the pamphlet, *Welcome in the Name of Christ*, published by the East Harlem Protestant Parish, p. 13.

16. *Only One Way Left* (Glasgow: The Iona Community Publishing House, 1956), p. 38.

17. (New York: Harper & Row, 1956.)

18. Gordon Cosby, "Not Renewal, But Reformation," in *Renewal*, April, 1963, p. 6. Used by permission.

19. From *The Service for the Lord's Day and Lectionary for the Christian Year.* Copyright © 1964, W. L. Jenkins. The Westminster Press. Used by permission.

20. Samuel H. Miller, *Prayers for Daily Use* (New York: Harper & Row, 1957), p. 27. Used by permission.

CHAPTER II

1. Emma Lazarus.

2. Robert B. Cunningham (editor), Division of Evangelism and Department of Urban Church, Board of National Missions, United Presbyterian Church in the U. S. A., 1961, p. 9.

3. *The Suburban Captivity of the Churches* (Garden City: Doubleday & Company, Inc., 1961); *The New Creation as Metropolis* (New York: The Macmillan Company, 1963).

4. (New York: Random House, 1961.)

5. Miller, *Prayers for Daily Use*, p. 121. Used by permission.

6. *Revolution in a City Parish* (Westminster: The Newman Press, 1949), p. 11.

7. George W. Webber, *God's Colony in Man's World* (Nashville: Abingdon Press, 1960), p. 32.

8. Information and filmstrips can be obtained from the East Harlem Protestant Parish. For address see Chapter IX.

9. Webber, *God's Colony in Man's World*, pp. 106-7.

10. *Parochial and Plain Sermons* (New York: Longmans, Green & Co., 1909), IV, 178.

11. George Appleton, *In His Name* (New York: St. Martin's Press, Inc., 1956), p. 100.

CHAPTER III

1. "Seeing the Unseen," in *The Christian Century*, March 25, 1964, pp. 387-88. Copyright 1964 Christian Century Foundation. Reprinted by permission from *The Christian Century*.

2. The Reverend and Mrs. Michael Hamilton, "Ministry to the Southern Mountaineer," mimeographed report, 1958. Italics mine.

3. *The East Harlem Protestant Parish*, one of six papers on church renewal (Nashville: the Board of Education of The Methodist Church, 1962), p. 5. Used by permission.

4. Sheila D. Woods, "A Cup of Cold Water," in the *International Journal of Religious Education*, January, 1963, p. 35.

5. *God's Colony in Man's World*, p. 86.

6. Janette T. Harrington, "New Days, New Ways," in *Presbyterian Life*, March 15, 1963, p. 9. Copyright 1963 by *Presbyterian Life*. Used by permission.

7. *Ibid.*, p. 10.

8. *Ibid.*, p. 38.

9. W. B. J. Martin, *Acts of Worship* (Nashville: Abingdon Press, 1960), p. 187.

10. Reinhold Niebuhr. Used by permission.

11. Martin Luther.

CHAPTER IV

1. *The Man Born to Be King* (New York: Harper & Row, 1943), p. 26.

2. "One Thing Worse Than This," in *The Christian Century*, December 11, 1963, p. 1555. Copyright 1963 Christian Century Foundation. Reprinted by permission from *The Christian Century*.

3. A letter from Ann Peyton to *The Christian Century*, December 18, 1963, p. 1588. Copyright 1963 Christian Century Foundation. Reprinted by permission from *The Christian Century*.

4. "A Report to Our Readers," in *Ladies' Home Journal*, April, 1964, p. 19.

5. *Ibid.*

6. "The Ignored Lesson of Anne Frank," in *Harper's Magazine*, November, 1960, p. 46. Part of the book, *The Informed Heart* (New York: The Free Press of Glencoe, Inc., 1960).

7. *The Christian Century*, April 16, 1941.

8. Charles Morgan, Jr., "Who Is Guilty in Birmingham?" in *The Christian Century*, October 2, 1963, pp. 1195-96. Copyright 1963 Christian Century Foundation. Reprinted by permission of *The Christian Century*.

9. "Rep. Green Blames Silence by 'Good' People as Encouraging Spread of Hate Mongers," in *The Sunday Oregonian*, December 1, 1963.

10. See his editorial "The Number One Question," in *Saturday Review*, July 28, 1951, pp. 20-21.

11. Reprinted from *Social Progress*, December, 1956. Copyright 1956 by the Board of Christian Education of the Presbyterian Church U. S. A. Used by permission.

CHAPTER V

1. From the *Post-Record*, Camas, Washington, September 19, 1963.
2. John Oliver Nelson (editor), *Work and Vocation* (New York: Harper & Brothers, 1954), p. 33.
3. *Ibid.*, p. 34.
4. *Ibid.*, p. 67.
5. George Herbert.
6. Sheila D. Woods in the *International Journal of Religious Education*, July/ August, 1963, p. 31. Title changed from "The Search," and other minor changes made.
7. J. Irwin Miller quoted in "Unity at the Golden Gate," by Harold E. Fey, in *The Christian Century*, December 21, 1960, p. 1504.
8. Gibbs and Morton, p. 70.
9. *Ibid.*, p. 64.
10. Facts found in the *Oregonian*, March 23, 1964, p. 7.
11. January 25, 1964, p. 4.
12. *Ibid.*
13. Percy Dearmer.
14. Letter to the editor in the *Wall Street Journal*, June 28, 1960.
15. Sheila D. Woods, "Take My Moments and My Days," in the *International Journal of Religious Education*, May, 1963, p. 33.
16. Martin, *Acts of Worship*, p. 185.
17. *Only One Way Left*, p. 142.
18. "Leisure, Blessing or Bane," in *Presbyterian Life*, August 1, 1962, p. 34.
19. Hazel Brownson. From *The Hymnal For Youth*. Copyright 1941 by The Westminster Press. Used by permission.
20. Ignatius of Loyola.

CHAPTER VI

1. Robert Montgomery, "Wanted: Christian Atheists," in *Hi Way Magazine*, August, 1964, pp. 6-7.
2. (Philadelphia: The Westminster Press, 1963.)
3. Donald A. Lowrie, "Children's Crusade in Reverse," in *The Christian Century*, September 16, 1964, p. 1143.
4. (Garden City: Doubleday & Company, Inc., 1961.)
5. *Ibid.*, p. 115.
6. Gerald Kennedy, "Aldersgate and 1963," in *The Christian Century*, May 22, 1963, p. 678.

7. Robert E. Fitch, "Sexplosion," in *The Christian Century*, January 29, 1964, pp. 136-38, Copyright 1964 Christian Century Foundation. Reprinted by permission from *The Christian Century*.

8. (Nashville: Abingdon Press, 1929.)

9. *The Book of Common Prayer*.

10. Harold E. Fey, "The Enemy Within," in *The Christian Century*, November 7, 1962, p. 1344. Copyright 1962 Christian Century Foundation. Reprinted by permission of *The Christian Century*.

11. Paul Dehn and Edward Gorey, *Quake, Quake, Quake* (New York: Simon and Schuster, 1961), p. 101.

12. Elizabeth O'Connor, *Call to Commitment* (New York: Harper & Row, 1963), p. 34.

13. Text published in *The British Weekly*, May 16, 1963.

14. Webber, *God's Colony in Man's World*, p. 139. Detail on Discipline also taken from this book.

15. Ibid., p. 142.

16. Francis of Assisi.

CHAPTER VII

1. Selections from the writings of Evelyn Underhill, arranged and edited by Douglas V. Steere (Nashville: The Upper Room, 1961), p. 17.

2. A prayer of the Iona Community.

3. Sheila D. Woods, "The Confusions of Mary and Martha," in the *International Journal of Religious Education*, April, 1963, pp. 32-33.

4. Gibbs and Morton, *God's Frozen People*, p. 11.

5. Robert Davy in a letter to *Women's Work*, October, 1963, p. 110. Used by permission.

6. From a report by Ruth Grob in *Presbyterian Life*, September 1, 1963.

7. *The Crisis of the World and the Word of God*, six Bible studies by Thomas C. Oden (Nashville: the Board of Education of The Methodist Church, 1962), p. 5.

8. Appleton, *In His Name*, pp. 118-19.

9. T. Ralph Morton, *Work and Worship in the Iona Community*, one of six papers on Church Renewal (Nashville: the Board of Education of The Methodist Church, 1962), p. 3.

10. *Only One Way Left*, pp. 37-38.

11. From *When We Pray*, Wilminer Rowland, copyright 1955, Friendship Press, New York. Used by permission.

12. John Baillie, *A Diary of Private Prayer* (New York: Charles Scribner's Sons, 1949), p. 93.

13. Oden, *The Crisis of the World and the Word of God*, p. 36.

CHAPTER VIII

1. *More Preaching Values in the Epistles of Paul* (2 vols.; New York: Harper & Row, 1961), II, 49-50.

2. Brian A. Wren, in a letter to the editor, *The British Weekly*, August 27, 1964. Used by permission.

3. Sheila D. Woods, "Praise God from Whom All Blessings Flow," in the *International Journal of Religious Education*, June, 1963, p. 32.

4. Raymond Crips, "Computers Instead of Cucumbers," in *The British Weekly*, May 23, 1963.

5. Margaret G. Hummel, "God in Their Own Lives," in the *International Journal of Religious Education*, January, 1964, p. 8. Used by permission.

6. *Letters from a Traveller* (New York: Harper & Row, 1962), p. 183*n*.

7. *Ibid.*, p. 111.

8. T. R. Morton, "Worship and Daily Life," in *The Coracle*, November, 1963, pp. 17-18.

9. *Ibid.*, p. 19.

10. Miller, *Prayers for Daily Use*, p. 39. Used by permission.

11. Dom Gregory Dix, *The Shape of the Liturgy* (Westminster, England: Dacre Press: A. & C. Black Ltd., 1954), p. 744. Used by permission.

12. Miller, *Prayers for Daily Use*, p. 108. Used by permission.

13. "Episcopalians: Muddling Through vs. Creative Outreach," in *The Christian Century*, November 27, 1963, p. 1462.

14. Harold J. Berman, "The Russian Orthodox Church." Reprinted from the February 18, 1963 issue of *Christianity and Crisis*, p. 19.

15. Peter Hammond, *Liturgy and Architecture* (New York: Columbia University Press, 1961), p. 156.

16. Roy Mackintosh, "What Does a Church Look Like," in *The British Weekly*, January 16, 1964.

17. "A City Is a Civilization," in *Cities and Churches*, edited by Robert Lee (Philadelphia: The Westminster Press, 1962), p. 74.

18. *Ibid.*

19. Fourteenth-century prayer.

20. Copyright 1962 Christian Century Foundation. Reprinted by permission from the July 25, 1962 issue of *The Christian Century* and by permission of the author.

CHAPTER IX

1. *The Coming Reformation* (Philadelphia: The Westminster Press, 1960), p. 133.

2. *1963 Minutes and Reports of the National Conference of the Methodist Youth Fellowship*, p. 3.

3. Ronald Beasley, "The Church in the Catacomb," in *The British Weekly*, March 10, 1960.

4. Norma Beatty, "Teen Center Scottish Style," in *Hi Way*, May, 1961, p. 20.

5. Gabriel Fackre, "Encounter—Mission in the World," in the *International Journal of Religious Education*, October, 1964, p. 6.

6. James Punton, "Festival Night Club," in *The British Weekly*, August 27, 1964, p. 10.

7. "Wanted Volunteers," in *Hi Way*, April, 1964, p. 13.

8. From a personal letter to the author.

9. "Notes on Good and Evil," in *Renewal*, October, 1964, p. 19.

10. Helmut Lehmann, "Reconciliation in Action," in *The Christian Century*, June 26, 1963, p. 824.

11. From the East Harlem Protestant Parish *Newsletter*, June, 1961. Used by permission.

12. 475 Riverside Drive, New York, New York, 10027. This is thirty cents a copy.

13. From a pamphlet of the Ecumenical Voluntary Service.

BIBLIOGRAPHY

BOOKS

Allan, Tom. *The Face of My Parish*. New York: Harper & Row, 1957. Lively account of renewal in a Scottish city.

Berger, Peter L. *The Noise of Solemn Assemblies*. New York: Doubleday & Company, Inc., 1961. Caustic criticism of irrelevance of the churches today, but with sound theological basis.

Bonhoeffer, Dietrich. *Life Together*. Translated by Olive Wyon. New York: Harper & Row, 1954. Very helpful book on the discipline of living together; good study for a retreat.

Kenrick, Bruce, *Come out the Wilderness*. New York: Harper & Row, 1962. Colorful story of the East Harlem Protestant Parish, with more emphasis on the people living there than the theological reasons for the work.

Kraemer, Hendrik. *A Theology of the Laity*. Philadelphia: The Westminster Press, 1959. A "must" for anyone concerned with the true understanding of laity.

Lee, Robert, editor, *Cities and Churches*. Philadelphia: The Westminster Press, 1962. Collection of readings on understanding urban churches, their future, and wide variety needed to suit variety of needs.

MacLeod, George F. *Only One Way Left*. Glasgow: The Iona Community Publishing House, 1956. Vigorous, and witty, call to men today to follow God out in the world, by the founder of Iona Community and one of earliest leaders of the movement toward renewal.

Michonnaeau, G. Abbé. *Revolution in a City Parish*. Westminster: The Newman Press, 1949. Interesting account of a Roman Catholic parish in working class Paris.

Morton, T. Ralph. *The Household of Faith*. Glasgow: The Iona Community Publishing House, 1951. An essay on the changing pattern of the church's life from New Testament days, through the centuries, and to the task today.

Morton, T. Ralph and Mark Gibbs, *God's Frozen People*. Philadelphia: The Westminster Press, 1965. Stimulating challenge to the "ordinary Christian" about the part he must play out in the world today.

Myers, C. Kilmer. *Light the Dark Streets*. Greenwich Conn.: The Seabury Press, 1957. Moving account of the work of an Episcopal priest with youth gangs in New York.

O'Connor, Elizabeth. *Call to Commitment*. New York: Harper & Row, 1963. The story of one of the most widely discussed churches in America today, the Church of the Saviour, Washington, D.C., and its utterly new concept of mission.

Raines, Robert A. *New Life in the Church*. New York: Harper & Row, 1961. Renewal in a local church through small groups leading to deeper commitment and a new understanding of the meaning of koinonia.

Spurrier, William A. *Ethics and Business*. New York: Charles Scribner's Sons, 1962. Excellent account of the problems of ethics today, and of the need to change laws that cannot be upheld or are out of date.

Southcott, Ernest. *The Parish Comes Alive*. New York: Morehouse-Gorham Company, 1956. An account of the first "house church" experiment in England.

Stringfellow, William. *A Private and Public Faith*. Grand Rapids: William B. Eerdmans Publishing Co., 1962. By a layman, most outspoken in his protest against the religiosity of religion today, and calling for a return to a simpler, but profound, way of Christian living.

Visser 't Hooft, William A. *The Renewal of the Church*. Philadelphia: The Westminster Press, 1957. A classic by one of the world's great religious leaders of today.

Webber, George W. *God's Colony in Man's World*. Nashville: Abingdon Press, 1960. One of the best accounts of East Harlem Protestant Parish, a colony that exists to witness, and whose ministers live, along with their families, side by side with the poor and the outcast.

―――. *The Congregation in Mission*. Nashville: Abingdon Press, 1964. A call to the churches to stop talking about "renewal," and do something, to realize that each congregation *is* mission and should be joining in God's task out in the world.

Williams, Colin W. *Where in the World?* and *What in the World?* New York: National Council of the Churches of Christ in the U.S.A., 1963, 1964. Two paper back books for use with study groups wishing to explore the changing forms of the church's witness. The first was in such demand that the second followed, with accounts of issues that arose, what is being done and can yet be done by congregations eager to move out into the world where God is.

Winter, Gibson, *The Suburban Captivity of the Churches.* Garden City: Doubleday & Company, Inc., 1961. Stimulating examination of the predicament of city churches, with some very new and different suggestions for their renewal.

————. *The New Creation as Metropolis.* New York: The Macmillan Company, 1963. Continuation of above. Both books for those who live in large city.

Wyon, Olive, *Living Springs.* Philadelphia: The Westminster Press, 1963. A small book, but with great detail on new religious movements in Europe, especially the many communities and disciplined groups.

RECOMMENDED BOOKS OF PRAYER

Appleton, George. *In His Name.* New York: St. Martin's Press, 1959. A very fine collection of prayers and Scripture for the church and the world, with emphasis on intercession and mission.

Fosdick, Harry Emerson. *A Book of Public Prayers.* New York: Harper & Row, 1959. Prayers for the world today, in the magnificent Fosdick language.

Miller, Samuel. *Prayers for Daily Use.* New York: Harper & Row, 1957. Much briefer prayers than the Fosdick above, characterized by great simplicity and beauty in phrasing.

PAMPHLETS

Russell, Letty, Clyde Allison, and Daniel Little. *The City, God's Gift to the Church.* New York: Board of National Missions, The United Presbyterian Church in the U.S.A., 1961. Varied accounts of work carrying out conviction in truth of title.

Six Study Papers on Mission of the Church. Nashville: The Board of Education of The Methodist Church, 1962. Really excellent collection on new movements, here and in Europe.

Catalog of helpful pamphlets published by the Anti-Defamation League of B'nai B'rith.

MAGAZINES

Concept and *Laity:* published by the World Council of Churches.

Renewal: published by Chicago Missionary Society. Fine articles and pictures attracting readers far beyond Chicago.

High Issues: good newssheet for high school students from Fellowship of Reconciliation, Nyack, N.Y.

The Coracle: Iona Community, 214 Clyde St., Glasgow, Scotland.

Newsletter: East Harlem Protestant Parish.

Image: Journal of the Ecumenical Institute, 3444 Congress Parkway, Chicago, Illinois 60624

MUSIC

The Hymn Society of America, 475 Riverside Drive, New York, New York 10027.

This Society has obtained and promoted 132 new hymns, chiefly within the last ten years. Many are hymns for youth, written for Youth Week, and their authors were under 30 years of age. Write for their catalog.

Routley, Erik. *Hymns Today and Tomorrow.* Nashville, Tenn.: Abingdon Press, 1964. With the renewal of the Church, hymns must be relevant too. "New eyes will have new ears behind them, and for these new ears we need a new music and a new hymnody."

—————. *Twentieth Century Church Music.* New York: Oxford University Press, 1964. Has an excellent section on "pop" music in church, folk mass, and other experiments, including the Passion-mime, *A Man Dies.*

FILMS ON CHURCH RENEWAL

Many fine films are available from the TV series, *Look Up and Live.* Most are available from Carousel Films, 1501 Broadway, New York, and are for rent. One describes the Taizé Community in France, another shows the congregation in Burlington, Va., which has no regular church building, while another shows youth groups reaching out to new forms of Christian experience in the world.

Each denomination has produced fine films on renewal lately, and a reliable critique of each can be found in the annual Audio Visual Resource Guide, along with rental information.

Films are also available from East Harlem Protestant Parish, and many can be obtained from TV programs.

INDEX

Abingdon Bible Commentary, The, 146
Academies, Evangelical, 172-75
Academies, lay, United States, 174
American Baptist Church, The, 57
Agape, the Waldensian Ecumenical Youth Center, 154
American Cancer Society, 149
Albina, Portland, Oregon, 58, 60
American Friends Service Committee, 41, 219
Anti-defamation League, 101
apathy, 97-99
Augustine, 34
automation, 66-67

Bad Boll, Germany, 172
Becket, 216-17
Benedict, Don, 61, 62
Bethlehem Church, Minneapolis, 209
Bettelheim, Bruno, 97
Bible, New English, The, 120
Birch, John, Society, 95
Black Like Me, 216-17
Bonhoeffer, Dietrich, 98, 151
Boiten, Rolf, Pastor, 153
Borrelli, Father, 153
Burns, Robert, 107

career, choosing a, 116-17
Chapman, Jo, 29
Children's Story, The, 94-95
Chisholm, Jo Ann, 210
Christ Church, Milwaukee, 82
Christian Cabaret, Australia, 212-13
Christian and politics, 52-53
Christianity and responsibility for suffering, 189-91

Christians and the conflicts today, 165-67
church: house, 63-64; building, 25-26; and laymen, 119-21; location, 23; and money, 124-26; new forms of, 42-44; and politics, 61-62, 67, 73-74; purpose of, 27, 37, 84; renewal of, 14-15; in work and industry, 114-15, 120, 126, 127, 173-75, 179-81
Church of Christ, United, 206
Church of God, 213
Church of the Saviour, Washington, D.C., 43, 155, 156, 158-59
Church World Service, 77, 79, 207
City, God's Gift to the Church, 52
city, inner: youth service work, 204-5, 207, 209, 210-12
Clavell, James, 94
coffeehouses: as a new movement, 205-9; "Catacomb, The," 205; "Cephas," 208; "Encounter," 205-6; "Ichthus," 206; "Loft, The," 217-18; "Potter's House, The," 156, 157
Coffin, William Sloane, Jr., 201
College, Reed, 59
Columba, 176, 178
Communion, Holy: the meaning of, 163, 194-96, 197; new forms, 217
communities, international, 204
community, meaning of, 63
community, in the church family, 23, 36, 59, 61-62, 71, 82
community, church and, 48-49, 170-72, 203
community, 127, 176-78

Congregational Christian Church, The, 57
Cosby, Gordon, 43, 157
Council of Churches, Greater Portland, 59
Cousins, Norman, 105-7
Coventry Cathedral, 40, 180, 213, 214
Crippled Children's Society, 210
Cumbernauld, Scotland, 36

Death and Life of Great American Cities, The, 54
Deputy, The, 103
Diary of Anne Frank, The, 96
disciplines, new within the church, 157, 158-61, 218
discrimination, 49-51, 61-62, 71, 75-76, 100-101, 105-7
Donne, John, 162
Dunfermline Abbey, Bible class, 160

East Harlem Protestant Parish, 15, 56, 61, 72, 80, 128, 160-61, 217
Ecumenical Institute, The, 218
Episcopalian, 180, 215
Episcopal National Council, 35
evangelism, new meaning of, 127-28
Evangelical United Brethren Church, The, 57

Faith In Life Experiment, 216
Family Service Unit, 210
Fellowship of Reconciliation, The, 152, 219
Festival, Edinburgh, 208-9
Festival Harvest, Industrial, 188-89
Firma House Community Center, 216
Foula, Scotland, 81
Franklin, Benjamin, 122, 123
Freedom from Hunger, Campaign, 81
Friends Service Committee, 152

Gallup Poll, 22
Geiger, Zachary U., 112
glory, meaning of, 184-86
God's Frozen People, 119, 120
"Good Samaritan Law," 74

Govan Parish Church, 47
guilt, corporate, 90, 102-4

Hamilton, Michael, 71
Harlem, East, 22, 38, 57, 217
Harper's Magazine, 97
hate, 62, 87-89, 92-93, 95-96, 213-14
Henze, Richard, 30-31
"High Issues," 219
Hochhuth, Rolf, 103
Holmes, William A., The Reverend, 90, 91
Honest to God, 136
Hospitality House, San Francisco, 211
hymn suggestions, 46, 69, 85-86, 110, 134, 183, 201-2

"Ignored Lesson of Anne Frank, The," 97
International Christian Settlement, 104
International Student Movement for the U.N., 221
International Christian Youth Exchange, 221
Iona Community, The, 48, 154, 161, 176-79
"Invest Your Summer," 119

Jacobs, Jane, 54
Jefferson High School, Portland, 59, 60
Jehovah's Witness, 181

Ken, Bishop, 200
Kennedy, President John F., 90, 91, 201
Kibbutz, Urin, 214
Kildrum, parish church, 36
King, Martin Luther, Jr., 70
Kirchentag, The, 154, 169-72, 216
Kirkridge, 218

Ladies' Home Journal, The, 94, 95
Law, Good Samaritan, 72-74
layman, meaning, 168-69, 174
Lee, Robert, 131
Leeds, England, 63
leisure, 129-32

"Litany for Justice and Good Human Relations, A," 108-10
"Look Up and Live," 218
Luther, Martin, 34
Lutheran, The American Church, 216-17
Luccock, Halford E., 186
Lutton, Mrs. Charles, 60

MacGregor, Geddes, 203
MacLeod, George F., 39, 48, 127, 154, 176, 177
Man Born To Be King, The, 89
"Man Dies, A," 209
Margull, Hans, 15
Mellon, William and Gwen, 153
Mennonites, General Conference of, 57
Meredith, James, 153
Methodist Church, The, 57, 212
Michonneau, Abbé G., 56
migrants, 66
Minear, Paul S., 114
Montgomery, Robert, 136
Morton, T. Ralph, 194
Myers, Kilmer C., Bishop, 197

National Council of Churches of Christ in U.S.A., National Parks Ministry, 220
National Student Association, The, 220-21
Nelson, John Oliver, 218
"Nes Ammim," Israel, 104, 215
New Creation As Metropolis, The, 54
Newman, John Henry, Cardinal, 63
Noise of Solemn Assemblies, The, 138
Northern Student Movement, The, 220-21

Oden, Thomas, 173
Old Trinity Church, New York City, 199
Operation Reconciliation, 214-15
Orthodox, Greek, 60, 180
Orthodox, Russian, 60, 180, 198
Osman, John, 199

parish, meaning of, 55-57
Parks, Rosa, 70
Pentecostal, 180
Phillips, J. B., 120
Phoenix at Coventry, 41
Pius XII, Pope, 103
poverty, 121-23
prayer, suggestions, 45, 68, 85, 133-34, 182, 200-201
Presbyterian Church of Ireland, 178
Poll, Gallup, 122
Presbyterian Senior Highs, 207
Presbyterian Church, United, in the U.S.A., 57, 180
Prinz, Joachim, Rabbi, 103
Protestant, 163-64, 207

Quakers, 210, 219

Reader's Digest, The, 54
reconciliation, German youth, 41, 180, 214
Reformed Church in America, 57
renewal, church, 34
"Report To Our Readers, A," 95
"Right Way to Save Our Cities, The," 54
Roman Catholic, 163-64, 180, 203, 207
Royden, Maude, 101
Ryland, Robert E., The Reverend, 82-84

Salvation Army, 180
Saturday Evening Post, The, 122
Saturday Review, The, 105
Schutz, Roger, 180
Schweitzer, Albert, 104
Scott, Mary, 82-83
Scripture suggestions, 44, 67, 84-85, 108, 132-33, 182, 200
service, being of, 118-19
sex, today, 140-42
Small, Cynthia, 213-14
Southcott, Ernest, Canon, 63, 153
St. George's West Church, Edinburgh, 208

St. Patricks Cathedral, New York
City, 199
Stevenson, Adlai, 122
Stringfellow, William, 153
Suburban Captivity of the Churches,
The, 54
Sunday, meaning, 113

Taizé Community, 179-81
tape recorder, use of, 18
Teilhard, de Chardin, Pierre, 154, 191
Termier, Pierre, 191
Together, 29, 31
Trueblood, D. Elton, 159
Turner, John, 29

Vinay, Tullio, 154
vocation, Christian, 22
von Thadden, Reinhold, 154, 170, 171,
172

WASP, 185
Waldensian, Ecumenical Youth Center,
154
Walker, Alan, The Reverend, 212
Weatherhead, Leslie, 136, 137
Webber, George W., 15, 38, 72, 80
Welch, Robert, 95
Wall Street Journal, The, 124
Westminster Church, Minneapolis, 209
Whittier, John Greenleaf, 81
Winant Volunteers, 220

Winter, Gibson, 54
Work and Worship in the Iona Community, 176-78
Work Camps, London Young Friends,
210-11
World Council of Churches, 163
Church World Service, 207
communion, 163
Ecumenical Voluntary Service Project, 209
Ecumenical Institute, 1958, 43
worship, 30
and art, 197-99, 213
meaning of, 192-94
new forms of, 38, 64, 216, 217
preparation for, 17-18
purpose for, 15, 27-28
Wycliffe, 48

Yeovil Industrial Order, 161
Yoke of Christ, The, 159
Youth Assembly, North American, 21
Youth Center, Ecumenical, 154
Youth Hostel, Coventry, 41
Young Friends Work Camps, London,
210
youth, concept of God today, 135-37,
138-39, 142-46
Youth Employment Service, 221
Youth Fellowship, Methodist National
Conference, 1963, 203-4
youth, sense of integrity today, 146-52